THE FAMILY Handyman FIX
REPAIR &
REPLACE

THE FAMILY Handyman. FIX REPAIR & REPLACE

UPGRADE YOUR HOME LIKE A PRO!

Reader's Digest

The Reader's Digest Association, Inc.
New York, NY | Montreal

A READER'S DIGEST BOOK

Copyright © 2012 The Reader's Digest Association, Inc.

FOR READER'S DIGEST
U.S. Project Editor: Kim Casey
Project Production Coordinator: Wayne Morrison
Senior Art Director: George McKeon
Executive Editor, Trade Publishing: Dolores York
Manufacturing Manager: Elizabeth Dinda
Associate Publisher, Trade Publishing: Rosanne McManus
President and Publisher, Trade Publishing: Harold Clarke

FOR THE FAMILY HANDYMAN
Editor in Chief: Ken Collier
Senior Editors: Travis Larson, Gary Wentz
Project Editor: Mary Flanagan
Associate Editors: Elisa Bernick, Mary Flanagan, Jeff Gorton
Senior Copy Editor: Donna Bierbach
Contributing Designers: Joel Anderson, Teresa Marrone
Contributing Copy Editors: Donna Bierbach, Peggy Parker
Art Directors: Vern Johnson, Becky Pfluger, Marcia Roepke
Photographer: Tom Fenenga
Production Artist: Mary Schwender
Office Administrative Manager: Alice Garrett
Financial Assistant: Steven Charbonneau
Admin. Editorial Assistant: Roxie Filipkowski
Production Manager: Judy Rodriguez
Contributing Editors: Spike Carlsen, Dave Munkittrick, Tom Dvorak, Rick Muscoplat, Duane Johnson, David
    Radtke, Brett Martin, Jeff Timm
Contributing Art Directors: Roberta Peters, Bob Ungar, David Simpson
Contributing Photographers: Tate Carlson, Ramon Moreno, Mike Krivit, Shawn Nielsen, Krivit Photography;
    Bill Zuehlke
Illustrators: Steve Björkman, Don Mannes, Gabe De Matteis, Paul Perreault, Mario Ferro, Frank Rohrbach III,
    John Hartman
Other Consultants: Charles Avoles, plumbing; Al Hildenbrand, electrical; Joe Jensen, Jon Jensen, carpentry;
    Dave MacDonald, structural engineer; William Nunn, painting; Dean Sorem, tile; Costas Stavrou, appliance
    repair; John Williamson, electrical; Les Zell, plumbing
Vice President, Publisher: Lora Gier

Library of Congress Cataloging in Publication Data is available upon request.
    ISBN 13: 978-1-60652-413-8

We are committed to both the quality of our products and the service we provide to our customers.
We value your comments, so please feel free to contact us.

The Reader's Digest Association, Inc.
Adult Trade Publishing
44 S. Broadway
White Plains, NY 10601

For more Reader's Digest products and information, visit our website:

www.rd.com (in the United States)

Printed in China

1 3 5 7 9 10 8 6 4 2

Contents

INTERIOR PROJECTS, REPAIRS & REMODELING

ELECTRICAL & HIGH-TECH

PLUMBING, HEATING & APPLIANCES

EXTERIOR MAINTENANCE & REPAIRS

INTRODUCTION

"If you only do what you know you can do, you never do very much."

—Tom Krause, motivational apeaker

Home improvement is a process of discovery. First there's the realization that something needs to be fixed, replaced, or upgraded. If this project is something you've tackled before, you're likely to feel that your experience is all you need to successfully complete the task again. But what if this is something new? Something you've never done before? Then you'll want some expert advice with step-by-step directions and clear photos and illustrations to help you ensure a fix and not a failure.

That's where *The Family Handyman* comes to the rescue! In *Fix, Repair & Replace* we've collected the most authoritative and up-to-date home improvement information. Whether you're interested in plumbing, tiling, woodworking, lawn care, insulating, or trim carpentry, you'll find it inside. Plus we've included Special Sections on painting cabinets as well as tools and skills.

And we bring this useful content to you with the help of our readers, consultants, and experts. Our readers submit materials for some of our most popular departments, including Great Goofs and Handy Hints. Our experts are out there every day repairing and improving homes—inside and out—and solving real-life problems. And we use the best architects, designers, illustrators, and photographers to deliver, safe solid advice.

As you page through this practical guide you'll find hundreds of hints, tips, and repairs along with dozens of projects designed for the do-it-yourselfer. But as you tackle these home improvement projects, you will find other things as well: a feeling of accomplishment, the knowledge that the job was done right, a "homier" home, and a few extra dollars in your wallet.

Best of luck with all your home improvement projects!

—The staff of *The Family Handyman* magazine

SAFETY FIRST—ALWAYS!

Tackling home improvement projects and repairs can be endlessly rewarding. But as most of us know, with the rewards come risks. DIYers use chain saws, climb ladders and tear into walls that can contain big and hazardous surprises.

The good news is, armed with the right knowledge, tools and procedures, homeowners can minimize risk. As you go about your home improvement projects and repairs, stay alert for these hazards:

Aluminum wiring

Aluminum wiring, installed in about 7 million homes between 1965 and 1973, requires special techniques and materials to make safe connections. This wiring is dull gray, not the dull orange characteristic of copper. Hire a licensed electrician certified to work with it. For more information visit inspectny.com/aluminum/aluminum.htm.

Spontaneous combustion

Rags saturated with oil finishes like Danish oil and linseed oil, and oil-based paints and stains can spontaneously combust if left bunched up. Always dry them outdoors, spread out loosely. When the oil has thoroughly dried, you can safely throw them in the trash.

Vision and hearing protection

Safety glasses or goggles should be worn whenever you're working on DIY projects that involve chemicals, dust and anything that could shatter or chip off and hit your eye. Sounds louder than 80 decibels (dB) are considered potentially dangerous. Sound levels from a lawn mower can be 90 dB, and shop tools and chain saws can be 90 to 100 dB.

Lead paint

If your home was built before 1979, it may contain lead paint, which is a serious health hazard, especially for children six and under. Take precautions when you scrape or remove it. Contact your public health department for detailed safety information or call (800) 424-LEAD (5323) to receive an information pamphlet.

Buried utilities

A few days before you dig in your yard, have your underground water, gas and electrical lines marked. Just dial 811 or go to call811.com.

Smoke and carbon monoxide (CO) alarms

Almost two-thirds of home fire deaths from 2003 to 2006 resulted from fires in homes with no smoke alarms or no *working* smoke alarms. Test your smoke alarms every month, replace batteries as necessary and replace units that are more than 10 years old.

As you make your home more energy-efficient and airtight, existing ducts and chimneys can't always successfully vent combustion gases, including potentially deadly carbon monoxide (CO). Install a UL-listed CO detector, and test your CO and smoke alarms at the same time..

Five-gallon buckets and window covering cords

Since 1984, more than 75 children have drowned in 5-gallon buckets. Always store them upside down and store ones containing liquid with the covers securely snapped.

According to Parents for Window Blind Safety, 367 children have died in the United States in the past few decades after becoming entangled in looped window treatment cords. For more information, visit pfwbs.org or cpsc.gov.

Working up high

If you have to get up on your roof to do a repair or installation, always install roof brackets and wear a roof harness.

Asbestos

Texture sprayed on ceilings before 1978, adhesives and tiles for vinyl and asphalt floors before 1980, and vermiculite insulation (with gray granules) all may contain asbestos. Other building materials, made between 1940 and 1980, could also contain asbestos. If you suspect that materials you're removing or working around contain asbestos, contact your health department or visit epa.gov/asbestos for information.

For additional information about home safety, visit homesafetycouncil.com. This site offers helpful information about dozens of home safety issues.

1 Interior Projects, Repairs & Remodeling

IN THIS CHAPTER

SPRAY-TEXTURE A DAMAGED CEILING

If your spray-textured ceiling is just dingy or stained, you can renew it with a coat each of sealer and paint. But if the texture is falling off or missing in spots, you'll have to reapply texture to fix the problem. For small areas, say less than a foot in diameter, you could try using an aerosol can of repair texture. But the patch is bound to stick out like a sore thumb. For the best results, you're better off respraying the entire ceiling. It's a messy job, but it's not hard to do. In fact, after you spray one room, you'll probably want to keep going. You can spray-texture unsightly plaster or smooth drywall ceilings, too. As with most jobs, the key is in the prep work, which is the time-consuming part, too. Once the room is masked off, the ceiling prepped and the texture mixed, it'll only take you about 15 minutes to spray the ceiling.

If any of the paper drywall tape is loose or the drywall is soft or damaged, you'll have to repair and sand these areas first. In addition to the putty knives and drywall joint compound for the repairs, you'll need a wide putty or taping knife for scraping, a roll of 1-1/2-in. or wider masking tape, enough painter's plastic to cover the walls, a gallon or two of primer/sealer, a bag of spray texture (enough to cover 300 to 400 sq. ft.), and a compressor and hopper gun. You can buy coarse, medium or fine texture. If you're matching existing ceilings, take a sample of the material with you when you buy the texture and ask for help matching it. Medium is usually the best choice and will match most ceilings. You can rent a compressor and hopper gun for about $30 for a half day or buy a hopper

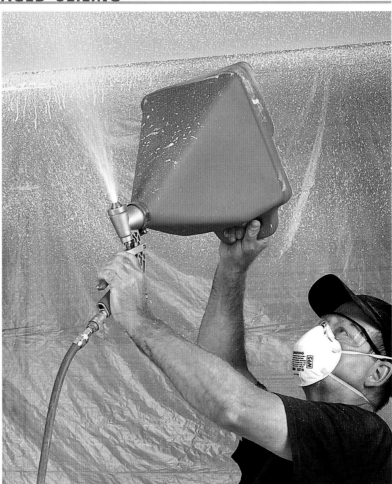

gun for about $70 and connect it to any average-size or larger compressor. If you use a small compressor, you may occasionally have to stop spraying to let the pressure build up. Minimize rental costs by getting all the prep work done before you pick up the compressor and hopper gun.

Start by removing everything you can from the room. If you must leave large furniture in the room, stack it in the center and cover it with plastic. Cover the floor with sheets or a canvas drop cloth. Then cover the walls with thin (1-mil or less) poly sheeting

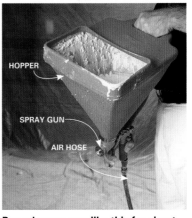

Buy a hopper gun like this for about $70 and connect it to any 2.5-cfm or larger air compressor.

LOOSE EDGE OF MASKING TAPE

PAINTER'S PLASTIC

1 Speed up and simplify your masking job by applying the tape along the ceiling first. Leave the lower edge of the tape loose. Then roll out a length of lightweight poly along the floor, pull one edge up to the ceiling and stick it to the tape.

2 Suit up with goggles, a dust mask and a hat before you start the messy job of scraping texture. Popcorn spray texture comes off easily if it hasn't been painted.

STAIN-SEALING PRIMER

3 Paint the ceiling with a fast-drying primer/sealer. Let it dry before applying the spray texture.

CAUTION: If you have ceiling texture applied before 1980, it may contain asbestos. Before you remove any ceiling texture, contact your state's department of environmental protection, department of health or a regional asbestos coordinator for information on asbestos testing and removal. For a list of contacts, go to epa.gov/asbestos/pubs/regioncontact 2.html#reg5. For general information on asbestos, go to epa.gov/asbestos.

(**Photo 1**). Painter's plastic is very thin and works great. Leave an opening with overlapping poly at the doorway so you can get in and out. Turn off the power to the lights and remove any ceiling fixtures. Don't forget to cap the bare wires with wire connectors. Stuff newspaper into the electrical box to keep out the spray texture.

The next step is to scrape off the old texture (**Photo 2**), but not before you've had it tested for asbestos. If it hasn't been painted, it'll usually come off easily. So try just scraping it first. If that doesn't work (you'll know right away), try wetting the texture with a pump-up garden sprayer. That might make it easier to scrape, but it'll leave a sticky mess on the floor. If you use this method, cover your drop cloths with 4-mil plastic so you can wad it up and dispose of the wet texture and not track it all over the house. Texture that's been painted over can be a lot harder to remove. Just do the best you can. Try to knock off the high spots and flatten it as much as possible. The ceiling doesn't have to be smooth, but it's easier to get a nice-looking job if most of the old texture has been removed.

When you're done scraping, paint the ceiling with stain-sealing primer (**Photo 3**). BIN and KILZ are two popular brands. Use an aerosol can of solvent-based sealer such as BIN white shellac to spot-prime severe stains. Then paint the entire ceiling with a water-based primer/ sealer.

The key to a successful spray-texture job is mixing the texture to the right consistency. Don't mix it too thick. Use the amount of water recommended on the bag as a starting point. Then adjust the thickness by adding more water or powder. Mix slowly using a mixing paddle mounted in a 1/2-in. drill (**Photo 4**). Mix thoroughly, adding water until the material reaches the consistency of runny yogurt—or thick paint—with tiny lumps in it. Let the texture sit for 15 minutes, then remix, adding more water, if necessary.

There are a few different versions of hopper guns, but they all have a mechanism at the nose that controls the diameter of the pattern, and a trigger control that helps govern the volume of spray. Start by setting both controls to the middle position. Then load the hopper about half full with texture material and practice on a piece of cardboard or drywall scrap (**Photo 5**). Adjust the spray pattern and trigger until you can get a nice, even pattern without runs or excess buildup. When you're comfortable with the spraying technique, start on the ceiling.

Start by spraying the perimeter (Photo 6). Hold the gun about 18 to 24 in. from the ceiling and aim so that about two-thirds of the spray hits the ceiling and the rest hits the wall. Move quickly around the room, paying special attention to the inside corners where walls meet. Remember, you can make another pass if it's too light. The goal is to cover the ceiling with an even layer of texture. Don't worry if it looks too smooth. The texture will become more pronounced as it dries. Be careful to avoid puddles. If you mess up and get a puddle or just a thick buildup, stop and scrape off *all* the texture with a wide putty knife. Then try again. Move the gun back and forth while backing up across the room. After you've covered the ceiling, turn 90 degrees and apply another light coat at a right angle to the first. Concentrate on filling in light spots to create an even texture.

When you're satisfied with the consistency of the texture, you can clean up the gun, hopper and hose with water and pull down the poly. If your masking job was a little off and there's texture on the wall or flooring, wait for it to dry. Then carefully scrape it off and remove the white residue with a wet sponge.

4 Mix the powdered spray texture and water thoroughly. Lumps will clog the spray tip and could mess up your spray job. Let it rest 15 minutes and remix, adding water, if necessary.

JUST RIGHT

TOO MUCH TEXTURE

5 Practice on cardboard or a piece of drywall to get a feel for spraying. Adjust the gun's tip and trigger until you get a consistent spray pattern that's easy to control.

6 Start by spraying the perimeter, then fill in the middle. Avoid heavy buildup—you can always add more.

JAMB LINER

SASH

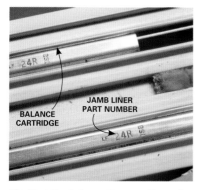

BALANCE CARTRIDGE

JAMB LINER PART NUMBER

LF 24R BS

LF 24R BS

1 Remove the sash. Push in on the jamb liner while you pull out on the top corner of the sash. Release the opposite side using the same technique. Then pivot the sash downward and tilt it sideways to remove it.

2 Pry out the jamb liner. Starting at the bottom, wedge a stiff putty knife into the crack between the jamb liner and the window stop. Pry the jamb liner flange out from under the stop. Then slide the putty knife upward to release the jamb liner.

3 Find the information you'll need to order new jamb liners stamped on the metal balance cartridges.

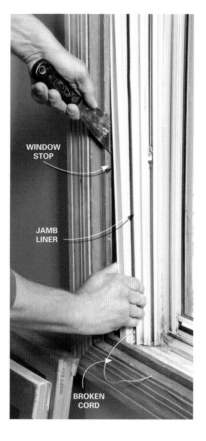

WINDOW STOP

JAMB LINER

BROKEN CORD

FIX A BROKEN WINDOW JAMB LINER

Modern double-hung windows (the upper and lower window sashes slide up and down past each other) don't use pulleys and sash weights to support the sash (the moving part of the window). Instead they have liners on each side that contain a spring assembly. If your sash won't stay in the raised position, chances are that some part of the jamb liner hardware is broken. You might be able to spot a broken cord or other sign of problem by looking closely as you open and close the window. If you determine that the jamb liner mechanism is broken, you can fix it by replacing both jamb liners.

The first step is to find a source for the new jamb liners. The original manufacturer is the best source of replacement parts. If you don't know your window brand and can't find a label, search online for a window repair parts specialist that can help you. Companies like Blaine Window Hardware at blainewindow.com (800-678-1919) can identify the jamb liner and send you new ones. But you may have to remove the jamb liner first and send in a sliver of it. Another option is to scan or photocopy the end profile of the jamb liner and e-mail the image to the parts supplier. Temporarily reinstall the old jamb liner and sash to secure the house while you're waiting for the new parts to arrive.

The photos show how to remove a common type of jamb liner on a Marvin window. **Photo 3** shows where to find the information you'll need to order a new Marvin jamb liner. Start by tilting out the sash (**Photo 1**). Then remove the jamb liner (**Photo 2**). If you're handy and want to save money, you can repair the jamb liner instead of replacing it. To see how, go to familyhandyman. com and search for "window repair."

HomeCare & Repair

CURE FOR CURLING VINYL

When water gets under the sheet vinyl along the edge of a shower or tub and the vinyl starts to curl, no amount of caulk can hide the problem. But here's an easy fix that also looks great. Buy a solid-surface threshold strip (Corian is one brand) at a home center or tile shop. They're available in various lengths and thicknesses; the one shown is 1/2 in. thick. The solid-surface material cuts like wood so you can use a handsaw or miter saw to cut the piece to the right length. **Photos 1 – 3** show how to complete the repair.

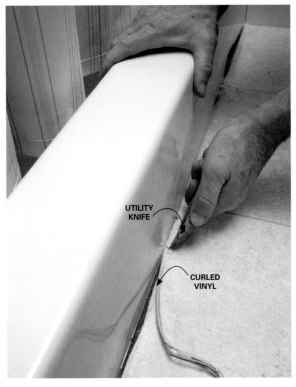

UTILITY KNIFE

CURLED VINYL

1 Cut out the curled vinyl. **Slice alongside the curled edge of vinyl flooring with a utility knife. Then peel off the thin strip of vinyl and clean out any dirt or old caulk.**

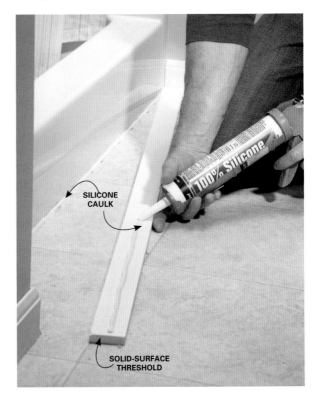

SILICONE CAULK

SOLID-SURFACE THRESHOLD

2 Attach a threshold. **Spread a bead of silicone caulk on the back of the threshold and along the base of the shower.**

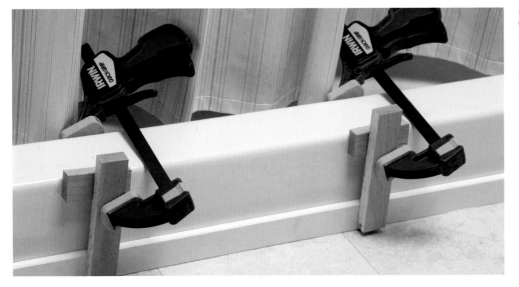

3 Clamp the threshold. **Press the threshold against the shower base. If there are gaps, use clamps to hold the threshold tight until the caulk sets.**

SUPER-INSULATE
YOUR ATTIC

Save $1,000 on labor and cut your heating bills

If you need to add insulation in your attic, save big by blowing in cellulose insulation yourself. The pros charge $1,500 to $2,000 to do a 1,200-sq.-ft. house. You can do it yourself for about $500. Blowing attic insulation isn't hard, but it's dusty, sweaty work. To make it easier, grab a helper and set aside two days: one for attic prep and the second to actually blow the insulation. By the end of the weekend you're going to be sore and tired. But saving $1,000 or more will make up for your aching back.

The long-term payoff is impressive, too. You could see your energy bills go down by as much as 15 to 25 percent depending on your climate and existing levels of insulation. And you can save an additional 30 percent on the cost of the insulation through the federal stimulus tax credit.

To show you how to do the job right, we asked our expert, Arne Olson, to share his tips for making the job go smoothly and help you avoid the top three attic-insulation mistakes.

DAY 1:

Seal attic bypasses

Leaks from cracks and gaps around lights, plumbing pipes, chimneys, walls and other ceiling penetrations are the equivalent of having a 2-ft.-wide hole in your roof.

The worst offenders are open stud and joist cavities and dropped soffits and ceilings in kitchens and baths. We'll show you some basics here (**Photo 1**), but for complete step-by-step detailed information about how to seal attic bypasses, go to familyhandyman.com and type "sealing attic air leaks" in the search box.

Install or repair vent chutes

"In 95 percent of the homes we work on, the vent chutes are missing or aren't properly installed," says Olson. Without them, you're not getting the most out of your insulation's R-value because air needs to move properly at the eaves to remove moisture in the winter and heat in the summer.

To make sure existing chutes aren't blocked, stand in a dark attic to see whether light from the eaves is filtering through the vents. Replace any chutes that are blocked, damaged or missing. You'll find both plastic and foam vent chutes ($1 each) at home centers. Olson recommends using foam chutes. "They're more rigid and there's less chance of them getting crumpled or compressed when you're installing them." Pull back the existing insulation so you can see out to the edge of the eaves, and install a vent chute in every rafter space (**Photo 2**).

1 Pull back the existing insulation and use expanding spray foam to seal any gaps around plumbing pipes, ceiling perforations and holes where electrical wires snake through. "Make sure to seal all the way around the pipe," says Olson. For gaps 1/4 in. or less, use caulk rather than expanding foam.

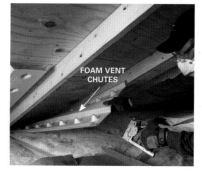

FOAM VENT CHUTES

2 Pull the existing insulation away from the roof. Position the new vent chute so the bottom extends 6 in. into the overhang and staple it into place. Olson suggests using a squeeze stapler instead of a hammer stapler. "It's more accurate and there's less chance you'll crumple the chute."

R-19 FIBERGLASS BATT

ATTIC HATCH

3 Cover the attic hatch with a pillow of fiberglass insulation. "You want a nice, big puffy pillow of insulation to stop any air leaks," says Olson. Cut two layers of R-19 fiberglass batt insulation slightly larger than the hatch and staple duct tape to the hatch edges to secure it in place.

Dam and insulate the attic access

To keep the insulation from falling through the attic hatch opening, make a 2x12 dam around the hatch perimeter. "Then, to really seal the attic access up tight," says Olson, "lay fiberglass batt insulation on the inside of the hatch or door and wrap it up tight like a Christmas present" (Photo 3). You can insulate the hatch door while you're inside the attic or slide the door out and do it more comfortably on a tarp outside.

Mark your final insulation level

When you're blowing insulation, it can get dusty and hard to see whether you've got it deep enough around the entire attic. Mark the desired level on different roof trusses around the attic before you start (Photo 4).

DAY 2:

Pick up the blower and insulation

Cellulose insulation is a good choice for DIYers. It has a higher R-rating and is less expensive than either blown fiberglass or fiberglass batts. It's an environmentally friendly material made from recycled newspaper, so it's easier on your skin and lungs. And you can blow it easily and quickly into odd-shaped spaces in an attic, where access is limited and dragging up batts is tough.

Most home centers sell bagged cellulose insulation ($6.75 per bag), and many provide the blower for a minimal fee ($20) or free when you buy a certain number of bags (usually 10 or more). You can also rent the blowers from a rental center for about $65 a day. Although rental machines aren't as powerful as the truck-mounted units the pros use, Olson says they work fine for a DIYer.

To determine how many bags you'll need, measure your existing insulation so you know your current R-value and subtract that from the recommended levels (see "Do You Need to Add Insulation?" below for how to find recommended levels for your ZIP code). Check the chart on

Do you need to add insulation?

The answer depends on where you live, the heating and cooling costs in your area, your existing insulation levels, local codes and more. The first step is to make sure you've sealed your attic bypasses. Then visit eere.energy.gov and go to "Calculators and Software," then "Homes," and the "Zip Code Insulation Tool." Use the insulation calculator to plug in your ZIP code, lifestyle factors, building design, energy costs and budget to get a detailed recommendation.

The recommended insulation level for most attics is R-38 (or about 12 to 15 in. from the drywall, depending on the insulation type). In the coldest climates, insulating up to R-49 is recommended.

4 Measure up from the ceiling to mark your desired insulation level. Use a permanent marker to mark the level every few trusses so you know you have even coverage around the entire space.

5 Have your assistant crumble the compressed cellulose as he loads the hopper so it doesn't clog the hose. If the cellulose comes out too fast or too slow, adjust the hopper door. The blower machine is loud, and you and your assistant won't be in visual contact. Communicate with each other using a walkie-talkie or cell phone. You can also click the blower control switch on and off several times to get your helper's attention.

6 Start at the farthest point from the hatch and sit in the center of the attic. "Don't move around a lot in the attic with the hose," says Olson. "Work from the middle and do three bays at a time." Push the hose out to the eaves and blow those areas first. Then pull the hose back and use a slow, steady sweeping motion until you reach the desired level. Then pivot in place and blow the opposite side of the attic the same way.

the insulation bag to determine the number of bags necessary to reach your desired R-value based on the square footage of your attic. Olson recommends buying more bags than you think you'll need. "You can always return them, and you don't want to stop in the middle of the job because you've run out."

Set up the blower

The blower machine is heavy, so have your partner along to help you load and unload it. Set the blower on a tarp on flat ground near the window or vent opening closest to the attic access. Your helper will feed the insulation into the hopper while you work the hose up in the attic (Photo 5).

The blower should include two 50-ft. hoses that you can connect and snake into the attic. If your hoses have to wind their way through the house to reach a scuttle (the attic access) in a hallway or closet, lay down tarps along the way. It keeps things neater during the process and makes cleanup a lot easier.

Connect the hoses with the coupler and then use duct tape over the coupler to secure the connection. "Those metal clamps can vibrate themselves loose," says Olson. "You don't want them to get disconnected and have cellulose sprayed all around your house."

Blow the insulation

Wear eye and hearing protection, a long-sleeve shirt and gloves, and a double-strap mask or particulate respirator. Start as far away from the access panel as possible and blow the eaves and other tight spots first. For hard-to-reach areas, duct tape a length of PVC pipe to the end of the blower hose. As you work back into corners and around eave vents, don't cover any ventilating areas.

You can blow three rafter bays on each side of the attic from one position. Let the hose sit on the drywall to fill the eave areas, giving it a shake to move it from bay to bay. For the center areas, hold the hose level and blow the insulation evenly until you've reached your level lines (Photo 6). Then pivot in place and do the same thing to the other side. Move across the attic until you've hit your desired height at every point. Blow the rest of the insulation until the hopper is empty. You'll end up with a clean blower, and the extra inch or two of insulation will settle over the next few months.

Our insulation expert

Arne Olson, the owner of Houle Insulation in Minneapolis (houleinsulation.com), has insulated more than 5,000 homes. "A lot of those homes were insulated by DIYers who didn't know what they were doing," says Olson. "They didn't use enough insulation and they didn't seal up the attic bypasses or put in vent chutes." Olson says it's also common for older insulation to settle over time. "But you can blow cellulose over whatever kind of insulation is already there, and this is a great DIY project for someone who doesn't mind working up a sweat."

THE 3 MOST COMMON DIY INSULATION MISTAKES

Mistake #1:
Not sealing attic air leaks first
"No amount of insulation is going to help if you don't seal your attic properly," says Olson. For detailed step-by-step information about sealing attic air leaks, go to familyhandyman.com and type "seal attic air leaks."

Mistake #2:
Not getting insulation out to the edges
"When you're prepping the attic, use a broom handle or stick to push the existing insulation out to the edges. Then when you blow in the cellulose, make sure you do a good job of getting it way over to the eaves with the hose."

Mistake #3:
Stepping through the ceiling
"It happens all the time," says Olson. "You've got to move around slowly and step from joist to joist." If there's no floor, bring up a 12-in.-wide piece of 3/4-in. plywood and lay it across the ceiling joists to use as a platform to work from. And wear rubber-soled shoes so you can feel the joists through the bottom of your feet.

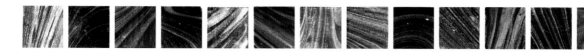

GLASS TILE **VANITY TOP**

A dramatic weekend face-lift

This vanity top would be at home in any luxury bathroom. Even though we chose relatively expensive glass tile, the completed top only cost us a little over $200, less than half the cost of custom granite, marble or solid-surface tops. Glass mosaic tile like we used is perfect for a project like this because you can adjust the size of the top to use only full tiles and avoid cutting. Plus you can choose from hundreds of colors, textures and patterns to create a look that's perfect for your décor.

You'll be able to finish this project in a weekend using standard carpentry tools and a 3/16-in. V-notch trowel, a grout float and a grouting sponge. A microfiber cloth works better than a cotton rag for cleaning off the grout haze. You can buy them at home centers, hardware stores and most discount retailers. You'll also need buckets for mixing thin-set and grout and for rinse water. Don't forget a pair of rubber, vinyl or latex gloves and safety glasses.

Round up the materials

Start by choosing the tile. (This could be the hardest part!) If your local tile shops or home centers don't have tile you like, shop online instead. Cooltiles.com is one source that offers an almost unlimited selection and reasonable prices. To duplicate this project, choose a 3/4-in. square mosaic that's 1/8 in. thick and has a mesh backing. Avoid mosaics that are held together with a removable paper face. They're difficult to install.

Plan to spend $7 to $24 per square foot for glass tile. Here's a list of other materials you'll need:

■ **Plywood.** We used two layers of 5/8-in. plywood, which, combined with the 1/4-in. backer board, resulted in a 1-1/2-in.-thick top, a perfect thickness for two courses of our 3/4-in. tile. If your tiles are a different size or you want a different top thickness, adjust the plywood and backer board thicknesses accordingly.

■ **Tile backer board.** We purchased Custom Building Products' EasyBoard (custombuildingproducts.com) from a local tile shop. EasyBoard is a lightweight tile backer board that you can cut with a utility knife. Hardibacker or any similar cement backer board would also work well.

■ **Thin-set mortar.** Look for special glass tile mortar.

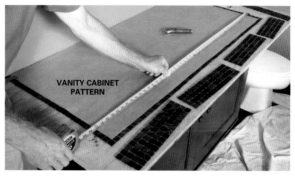

1 Design the top to avoid cutting tile. **Cut a paper pattern the size of the vanity cabinet and lay it over the tile.** That makes it easy to size the top for full tiles.

2 Build the plywood base. **Two layers of plywood make a stiff, strong base for the tile. Mark and cut the plywood** carefully to make sure the top is perfectly square.

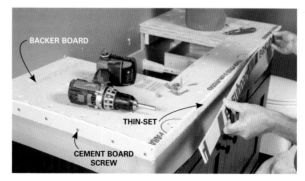

3 Cover the base with backer board. **Tile backer board forms a waterproof layer for a long-lasting countertop.** Quarter-inch-thick backer is all you need over the strong plywood base.

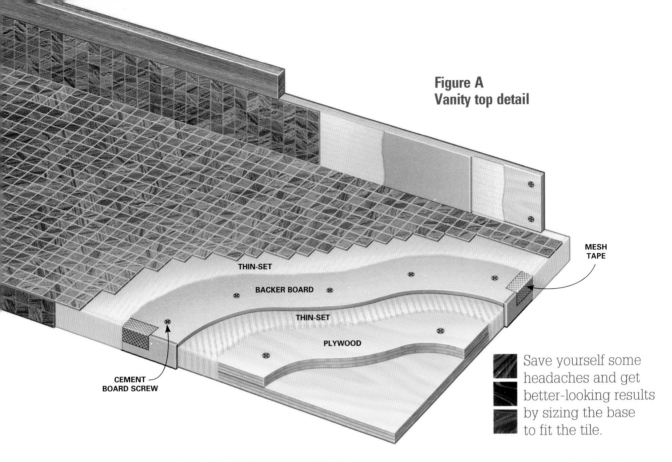

**Figure A
Vanity top detail**

THIN-SET

BACKER BOARD

THIN-SET

PLYWOOD

MESH TAPE

CEMENT BOARD SCREW

Save yourself some headaches and get better-looking results by sizing the base to fit the tile.

FLATTENED THIN-SET

4 **Comb out, then flatten the thin-set.** Use a 3/16-in. V-notch trowel to spread a layer of thin-set over the backer board. Then flatten it with the straight side of the trowel.

LINE UP GROUT SPACES

5 **Start setting the tile at the corner.** For perfectly aligned grout joints, start by setting a strip of tile on the front and side edges, and a full sheet of tile on top. Adjust the tile until the grout lines on the top line up with the grout lines on the front and sides.

It's white and specially formulated to stick well to glass tile. It's available in a powder that you mix with water. Standard modified white thin-set will also work.

■ **Cement board screws.** Choose screws that are labeled for use with cement board. They have a special corrosion-resistant coating.

■ **Cement board tape.** Check the label—it must be cement board tape so the mesh will hold up to the alkaline cement products.

■ **Grout.** We used nonsanded grout because we wanted smooth grout lines. You can also use sanded grout. Make a sample board by gluing a few glass mosaic tiles to a scrap of wood and grouting them to make sure you like the result.

Size the base

Glass tile is a nightmare to cut. Save yourself some headaches and get better-looking results by sizing the base to fit the tile. With the tile in hand, you can figure out exactly what size to build the plywood base. One easy method is to carefully lay out the sheets of mosaic with an equal grout space between the sheets. Make a paper pattern of your vanity cabinet including the thickness of the door or drawer fronts. Arrange the pattern over the sheets of tile and adjust the position until there's an equal-width tile on each side. Use the pattern to determine the overhangs, based on where full tiles occur. Aim for about a 1/2-in. overhang on the sides and between 1/2-in. and

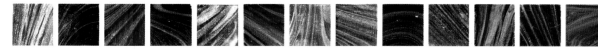

1-in. past the drawers on the front. Cut the mesh backing so the sheets of tile are the size of the top. Now carefully measure the width and length of the tiles. This will be the finished size of your countertop after it's tiled.

The plywood base has to be smaller than the size of the finished top to accommodate the backer board, tile and thin-set. To figure the size of the plywood, add the thickness of the tile (1/8 in.), the tile backer board (1/4 in.) and the thin-set (1/16 in.) and subtract this amount from the width (front to back). Deduct twice this amount from the length (side to side). It's critical that you cut the plywood to exactly the right size, so double-check all your math (Photo 1).

Build the base

Cut both layers of plywood, being careful to make exact cuts. Then plan the sink location and make the sink cutout. Self-rimming sinks usually include a template that you can use to trace the cutout onto the plywood. Cut the backer board to the same size as the plywood and make the sink cutout. You'll also need strips of backer board to cover the edges.

Screw the two layers of plywood together. Space screws about 8 in. apart. Then screw the plywood to the vanity cabinet, making sure the overhang is even on both sides and that the front edge is parallel to the vanity cabinet (Photo 2).

Next cover the plywood with backer board (Photo 3). Cut and test-fit the backer board first. Then mix powdered thin-set mortar with water to about the consistency of peanut butter. Spread it onto the plywood with a 3/16-in. V-notch trowel. Finally, screw the backer board to the plywood, placing screws about 8 in. apart.

The last step before tiling is to wrap the corners of the backer board with cement board tape. Start by vacuuming and then wiping the top and edges with a clean cloth to remove dust. Wrap the adhesive-backed tape around the

corners and press it down. Then cover the tape with a thin layer of thin-set mortar. After the thin-set hardens, scrape off any lumps and dust off the top again to prepare it for tiling.

6 Embed the tile with a wood block. **Tap the top of the mosaic tile with a flat block of wood to level the surface and ensure a secure bond with the thin-set.**

FLAT WOOD BLOCK

GROUT FLOAT

7 Grout the tile. **Work the grout back and forth in different directions to completely fill the joints and eliminate voids. Well-packed joints are the key to a lasting grout job.**

Glass tile mirror

The mirror frame is made from a 3/4-in. x 4-1/2-in. oak board with a 1-5/8-in.-wide dado on the face to accommodate a band of tile and a 3/8-in. rabbet on the back to hold the mirror. We cut the dado with dado blades mounted on a table saw. A router would also work. We sized the frame so we wouldn't have to cut tiles at the corners. After mitering the parts and staining the frame, we set the tile strips in a thin bead of construction adhesive. Then we finished it off by masking the wood and grouting the tile.

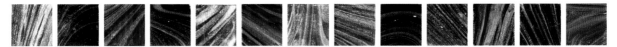

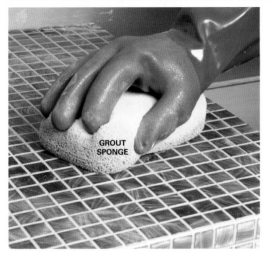

8 "Tool" the grout with a damp sponge. **Wait until the grout starts to set up before tooling. Wring out the sponge until it's just damp. Then rub it over the tile in a circular motion to smooth and shape the grout and fill tiny voids and pinholes.**

9 Buff off the grout film. **Wait until the grout is hard before buffing it. Then polish it with a microfiber cloth to remove the haze.**

Buyer's Guide

- **TILE:** HotGlass Aventurine blended 3/4-in. glass tile in Tiger's Eye Blend on mesh-backed sheet. $19 per sheet (HAK-34313). Available online from cooltiles.com.
- **SINK:** Elements of Design, Mission Bathroom Sink (EDV9620-black), $280. Available online at everyvesselsink.com.
- **FAUCET:** Price Pfister Kenzo single-center faucet (T42-DF0), $195. Available online at everyvesselsink.com.

Tile the countertop

Photos 4 – 6 show how to spread the mortar and embed the tile. Before you start, cut the mesh backing to form strips of tile for the edges and make the sink cutout. Trim the mesh tight to the tile so you don't have any mesh whiskers sticking out. Then arrange the tile in the shape of the vanity and within easy reach of the vanity top so you can easily reach it after spreading the thin-set.

Mix and spread the thin-set. Pay close attention to **Photo 4**; it shows an important tip. Flattening the mortar after you spread it with the notched trowel prevents thin-set from filling the grout spaces when you embed the tile. Any thin-set that gets into the grout spaces has to be cleaned out before you can grout the tile, so this tip will save you a lot of time and effort.

Set the tiles on the top and edges as quickly and accurately as possible (**Photo 5**). You need to work fast so you can make slight adjustments to the tile before the thin-set starts to set up. When you're satisfied that the tile top and edges are perfectly aligned, embed the tile (**Photo 6**). Let the thin-set harden overnight before grouting.

Grout the tile

Photos 7 – 9 show how to grout the tile. Start by mixing the grout according to the directions on the package. Let it rest for about 10 minutes—this is called "slaking." Then mix it again. It'll often thicken a bit after slaking and require a bit more water. The grout should be the consistency of mayonnaise.

Here are some grouting tips:

- Work the grout from all angles with the float to completely fill the joints (**Photo 7**).
- Scrape off the excess before it starts to set.
- Wait until the grout starts to harden before cleaning it with a sponge. If you can't make a fingerprint, it's hard enough.
- Keep the rinse water clear and wring all the water out of the sponge when you're cleaning the grout. Use a clean side of the sponge for each cleaning stroke.
- Use a damp sponge to tool the grout after it sets up (**Photo 8**). Wait about 15 minutes after cleaning before tooling the tile.
- Coat the grout with a grout sealer to help prevent staining and make it more water-resistant. Wait two or three days before sealing.

Finishing touches

We added a backsplash before setting the sink. A backsplash could be as simple as tiles attached to the wall with thin-set, or something more elaborate. We screwed 3/8-in. plywood to the wall, covered it with 1/4-in. backer board and surrounded it with 3/4-in.-thick oak trim. Then we tiled over the backer board, grouted the tile and caulked the seam between the countertop and the backsplash with a fine bead of clear silicone caulk.

Do's&Don'ts

TIPS FOR **TIGHT MITERS**

There are perfect miters—and then there are miters that have been tweaked to look perfect. You can learn how to do both with the right tools, a few pro tips and a good dose of patience. We can't help you with the patience, but we can show you tips and techniques for cutting, fitting and joining perfect miters, along with a few tricks for making those less-than-perfect miters look their best.

Make sure your blade is sharp

Choosing the right blade for your miter saw, and making sure it's sharp, are crucial for cutting tight-fitting miters. You can't cut perfect miters with a dull blade, one with too few teeth or one that's designed for ripping. Check your blade for sharpness by cutting a 45-degree miter on a 1x3 or larger piece of oak or other hardwood (**photo below**). If the blade cuts smoothly with very little pressure and leaves a clean, almost shiny cut with no burn marks, it's sharp enough to cut good miters.

When you check your blade or shop for a new one, here's what to look for. First, it should be labeled as a "trim" or "fine crosscutting" blade. A 10-in. blade should have at least 40 teeth, a 12-in. blade at least 60. If the blade is for a sliding miter saw, be sure the teeth have a hook angle of zero to negative five degrees. Teeth with a neutral or negative hook angle are less aggressive and safer for sliding miter saws. Expect to spend at least $50 for a carbide-tipped blade that'll perform well and last.

SHARP BLADE

TEAROUT

If the cut end of the miter looks scorched, rough or chipped, have the blade sharpened or buy a new one.

DULL BLADE CUT

SHARP BLADE CUT

Guess and test

There are all kinds of ways to find odd angles, but most carpenters simply make a guess and then cut a pair of test pieces to see how lucky they are. The angle of these two walls looks to be less than 45 degrees. A good guess would be about 30 degrees. Divide 30 by two to arrive at the miter angle, and cut a couple of scraps at 15 degrees. Here there's a gap in front, so we need to increase the angle slightly and recut the scraps at 16 degrees. When you've zeroed in on the correct angle, the scraps will fit perfectly, and you can then cut the actual moldings.

Cut test pieces to check the angle of the miter.

Do's&Don'ts

Tweak the cut

Even on perfectly square corners, 45-degree angles won't always yield perfect miters. Wall corners can be built up with corner bead and compound, and window and door frames can slightly protrude or be recessed behind surrounding drywall. That's when you have to start fiddling with the angles to get a tight fit.

In most cases, you'll be making adjustments as small as a quarter of a degree. If the gap is small (about 1/16 in.), recut one side of the miter (**Photo 2**).

If the gap is larger, you'll have to recut both boards or the trim profiles won't line up. For more tips, go to familyhandyman.com and type "tight miters" into the search box.

1 Cut the moldings at a 45-degree angle. Hold the miter together to see how it fits. If there's a gap, estimate how much you'll have to trim off to close the gap, and make a mark where the moldings touch.

2 Push the trim tight to the blade and adjust the angle of the saw until the gap equals the amount you need to trim off the miter.

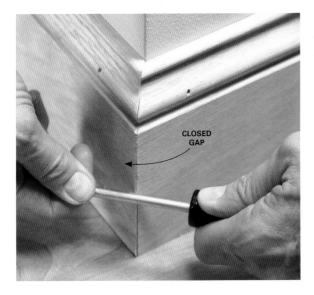

CLOSED GAP

Burnish the corner

You can make less-than-perfect miters on outside corners look their best with this tip. If your baseboard or crown molding has a slight gap in the outside corner miter, you can hide it by rubbing the tip of the miter with the shank of a screwdriver or nail set. The bent fibers will disguise the gap, and the slightly rounded corner will be less likely to get chipped or damaged.

The best way to prevent this problem is to cut your outside corner miters about 1 degree sharper than the actual angle so the tips of the miters touch. This will leave a tiny gap at the back of the miter where it's barely noticeable.

Hide a slight gap in an outside corner miter by rubbing it with the shank of a screwdriver or nail set. This will bend the wood fibers in and slightly round the corner.

Fit one miter at a time

Whether you're edge-banding a tabletop as we're showing here, trimming out a window or door or installing base-board, it's always best to fit one miter at a time whenever possible. Start with a scrap of molding with a miter cut on it as a test piece (**Photo 1**). When you have the first miter fitting perfectly, mark the next one (**Photo 2**). Then cut and fit the adjoining miter before you nail either piece. For edge banding, work your way around the project using the same process for each edge piece.

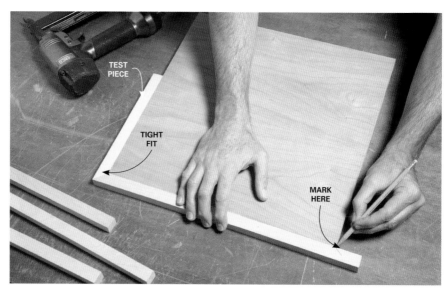

Tack a mitered scrap of edging to one side. Use it to hold the first edging piece in position. Hold the mitered end tight to the mitered scrap while you mark for the opposite miter.

Glue and sand for a seamless fit

Here's a trick to make miters look great, but it only works if you're installing raw trim that will get finished after installation. It's easy. Glue the joint, then sand it smooth.

The sawdust from sanding will mix with the glue to fill any small gaps. Sanding the miter will also even out any slight level differences and make the job look more professional. Don't try to fill large gaps, especially in trim that'll be stained. Glue-filled gaps absorb stain differently than the surrounding wood and will stick out like a sore thumb.

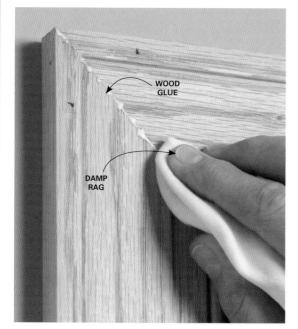

1 Apply a thin layer of wood glue to the end grain of each piece before you assemble them. Use a damp (not wet) cloth to remove excess glue from the joint.

2 Sand over the miter with a small piece of 120-grit sandpaper. Sand across the joint and finish up by carefully sanding out any cross-grain sanding marks by moving the paper with the grain from both directions.

Question&Answer

HOW TO SAVE A FLOODED BASEMENT

My basement flooded and I've got wet carpet. Is it possible to save it?

You didn't give us much info to go on, so you'll have to go by these rules: If the floodwater was clean (broken pipe, burst washing machine supply hose or a foundation leak), you can probably save the carpet (the pad is "iffy"). But you've got to act fast. If the carpet isn't dry within 72 hours, it'll start to grow mold. However, if the floodwater was dirty (sewer back-up or washing-machine-drain water), you need to call in the pros (see "Call in the Pros," p. 27).

We'll assume the basement was flooded with clean water, the water is now shut off and the cost of the carpet is less than your insurance deductible (or that you simply want to do it yourself to avoid a claim). Before you set one boot on that squishy carpet, heed this warning: You must turn off the power to the basement. If you're not positive which breakers power the basement receptacles, flip the main circuit

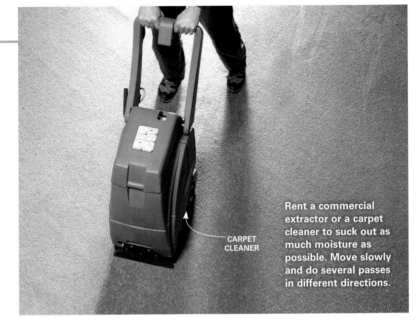

CARPET CLEANER

Rent a commercial extractor or a carpet cleaner to suck out as much moisture as possible. Move slowly and do several passes in different directions.

breaker in the garage panel. If your electrical panel is in the basement, *call an electrician to turn off the power.*

Next remove any extension cords and power strips from the floor and unplug or switch off all electrical appliances (washer, dryer, HVAC). Ask the electrician (if you hired one) to repower the upstairs (to keep the fridge going) and inspect the basement receptacles to determine whether it's safe to repower them. If not, you'll have to buy several GFCI-equipped extension cords and run power from upstairs receptacles.

Then it's time to extract the water from the carpet. Don't waste your time with a wet/dry shop vacuum—it simply doesn't have enough power. Instead, rent an extractor (if available) or carpet cleaner (shown; $65 per day), an air mover fan or two ($42 per day) and a large commercial

Save your stuff

Most people leave their valuable items in the basement while they dry out the carpet. Big mistake. The longer your items sit in the basement, the more moisture they'll soak up. And that means mold. So get them out of the basement fast!

- **Move all electronic gear upstairs (high humidity can corrode electronic components.)**
- **Take photos and artwork off the walls and move them to a dry location.**
- **Place valuable wet books in your freezer until the "freeze-drying" effect removes all the water from the pages.**
- **If you can't move furniture out of the basement, place aluminum foil under the legs.**

COMMERCIAL DEHUMIDIFIER

COMMERCIAL AIR MOVER FAN

Rent a commercial dehumidifier and air mover fan ASAP. Position the machines on opposite sides of the room to pick up and remove most of the moisture.

dehumidifier ($100 per day; see p. 26). Rent the largest dehumidifier available. The big ones can remove up to 30 gallons per day, compared with 4 gallons for the largest home units.

Extraction is 1,200 times more effective than dehumidification. You'll want to move the extractor slowly across the carpet to suck up as much water as possible. Don't rush this step! Once the water is out, peel back the carpeting (watch out for those rusted sharp nails on the tackless stripping) and remove the wet pad. Cut the pad into strips, roll it up and haul it outside. If the weather is hot, dry and sunny, you can try drying it yourself by rolling it out on your driveway. If that works, you can reinstall it by taping it back together. Just be aware that new carpet pad is cheap, so don't waste a lot of time trying to dry the old stuff.

Lay the carpet back on the floor and fire up the air movers and rental dehumidifier. Keep the basement temperature at or below 75° F. You might think hotter is better because it will dry everything faster. But a higher temp will accelerate bacterial growth and turn your basement into a petri dish.

While the carpet is drying, check the condition of the wall insulation. If you don't have insulation and you dry out the basement quickly, you don't have to replace the drywall. But if the insulation is wet, it's got to go (wet insulation cannot be saved). Snap a chalk line, cut the drywall with a recip saw and toss the wet stuff. Replace the insulation and install new drywall.

Finally, if your appliances or furnace was under water, call in appliance and HVAC specialists before plugging any of them back in.

Call in the pros

If you had a sewer backup, washing-machine-drain water spill or river flood, you need professional help. Pros are the only ones with the proper equipment to get your basement dry and disinfected in the shortest possible time.

To find a certified water restoration professional, check the yellow pages under "Water Damage Restoration" or search online. Look for IICRC (Institute of Inspection, Cleaning and Restoration Certification) credentials in the company's description (Servicemaster is one company that is fully certified). Or go to iicrc.org and click on "Locate a Pro."

Be aware that pros can give you a rough price estimate (the average cost of a basement cleanup is $2,500), but the final cost depends on how long it takes them to dry out your basement. There are just too many variables beyond their control (inside and outside temperature and humidity levels) to give you a set price up front. Be wary of any company that gives you a set price over the phone.

MATCH CAULK TO GROUT COLOR

I tiled and grouted my bathtub walls and went to the home center to buy caulk for the inside corners and tub ledge. I couldn't find anything that matched the sanded grout texture or color. Can I order it somewhere? Help!

Don't look in the caulk department; look for sanded caulk near the grout in the tile department. You'll find caulk that matches most grout colors, both sanded and unsanded. If the store doesn't carry it, or you have an unusual color, you can custom mix your own (**Photo 1**). You'll have to use a makeshift applicator (**Photo 2**) and it will be messy—so tape off the gap. Practice squeezing the bag on a piece of cardboard until you get a feel for how much comes out. Then squeeze out the caulk/grout mix and smooth with your finger.

CAULK AND GROUT MIXED

1 You can color the caulk with grout. **Squeeze caulk onto a mixing board, making sure you use enough to complete the entire job** (it'll be hard to match if you have to add more later). Then add colored grout to the caulk and mix thoroughly with a 3-in. putty knife.

2 It's like decorating a cake. Scoop a hefty portion into a zip-top freezer bag. Zip the top shut and snip off one bottom corner. Then apply the caulk/grout bead to your tub and tool the joint with a plastic spoon or wet finger. Then pull the tape free before the caulk sets up.

Question&Answer

SEAL EXPANSION GAPS ON LAMINATE FLOORING IN WET AREAS

I bought AC3-rated laminate flooring for my bathroom because it's a wet area. But now I'm confused about the expansion gap. The instructions say to leave a 1/4-in. gap along the wall. Won't water get in there and defeat the whole purpose of buying water-resistant flooring?

Anytime you install laminate flooring in a bath, laundry room or kitchen, you should fill gaps at flooring ends with 100 percent silicone caulk. It stays flexible, allowing the floor to expand, and in the event of a spill, prevents water from soaking into the laminate core. Filling the gaps can use up a lot of caulk, so buy more than you think you'll need.

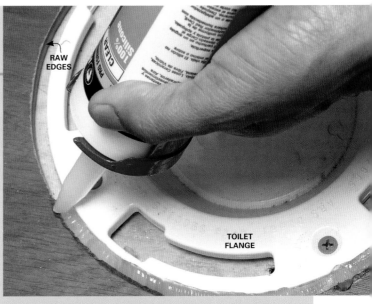

RAW EDGES

TOILET FLANGE

Hold off on setting the toilet and the baseboard molding until you've filled the expansion gaps around room perimeters and the toilet flange with 100 percent silicone caulk.

CEILING FAN REMOTE RETROFIT

I have an old ceiling fan and light that operates via pull chains. Can I retrofit it with a remote control?

Probably. There are many "universal" remote kits on the market ($20 to $80). All of them feature on/off and fan speed control. Others also offer light-dimming and thermostatic control capabilities. But whether you can use a kit depends on the amount of free space inside the fan canopy.

Many "ceiling hugger"–style fans have enough free space for the receiver. But "down-rod" styles may not.

FAN CANOPY

1 Slide the receiver into the space above the down rod. If it doesn't fit, try other locations inside the canopy.

Shut off the circuit breaker to the fan and lower the canopy (use a voltage sniffer to make sure the power is really off). Check the fit of the receiver before you commit to wiring it in permanently. Keep your receipt just in case.

With the power off, connect the hot and neutral wires to the "AC-in" wires on the receiver. Then connect the three remaining wires to the fan and light (they're labeled by the manufacturer).

If you have neighbors nearby, you may have to change the frequency on the transmitter and receiver to prevent you or your neighbors from controlling one another's fans (see Photo 2).

2 Flip the DIP switches to change the transmitter frequency if you have problems with interference. The switch positions on both units must match.

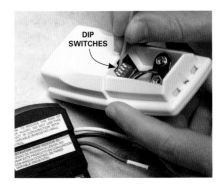

DIP SWITCHES

DIY SOLID-SURFACE COUNTERTOPS?

I'm pretty handy, and I'd like to install a solid-surface countertop myself and hopefully save a boatload of money—if that's possible. Is this a DIY project and where would I buy the stuff?

Yes, it's possible and there are sources that will sell to DIYers. But only if you're talking about the acrylic material (like Wilsonart, Avonite and Meganite), rather than "engineered stone" (quartz/resin) products like Cambria and Silestone. Engineered stone materials are only available through authorized dealers and are custom made for each job.

DIYers can buy solid-surface materials at wholesale prices from solidsurface.com. It sells surplus and discontinued sheets from several major manufacturers. Full-sheet sizes vary but are usually 30 in. x 144 in. x 1/2 in. (partial sheets are half that size). The square-foot prices vary by pattern and manufacturer, ranging from $10 to $20 per sq. ft. plus shipping ($150 to $300, depending on your location). The total is about one-third of what you'd pay an authorized dealer if it would even sell to you. Solidsurface.com also carries the special adhesives you'll need for the joinery. And you'll have to spend about $250 for special tools and materials (see photo).

It's possible to do the installation yourself if you've built a cabinet or two or are an intermediate woodworker. Solid-surface materials can be cut and routed just like wood. Use sharp, carbide-tipped bits and blades so they cut cleanly through the material instead of heating it up and melting it.

The supplier provides great instructions on its Web site, but here's the routine in a nutshell. Simply rip the sheets with a table saw or circular saw and straightedge to get the 4-in. backsplash and the 1-in. front lip. Then apply the adhesive to the front lip and clamp the pieces together for 30 minutes. Use the special router bit (with a nylon bearing) to rout a decorative edge. Then lay down 3/4-in. plywood over your existing cabinets and install the new countertop. Glue the backsplash and seams and sand them with the special discs.

ADHESIVE GUN

ADHESIVE

ABRASIVE DISCS

ROUTER BIT

ADHESIVE NOZZLE

ABRASIVE DISCS

Besides your countertop material, you'll need a two-part adhesive gun, adhesive, router bits and abrasives to fit an orbital sander. Then use your regular woodworking tools to rip and crosscut the solid-surface material.

Question& Answer

PREP CONCRETE FOR TILE

OLD ADHESIVE

1 Scrape off as much of the adhesive residue as possible with a razor scraper. If any leftover adhesive is sticky, loosen it with a chemical adhesive remover.

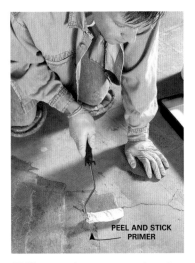

PEEL AND STICK PRIMER

2 Vacuum the area around cracks and apply a "peel-and-stick" primer with a roller or paint pad.

CRACK ISOLATION MEMBRANE

3 Apply a layer of crack isolation membrane over cracks to prevent cracks from appearing later in the overlying tile.

The vinyl tile in my basement is in bad shape, and I want to replace it with either ceramic or porcelain. How do I get the old tile off and prep the concrete for new tile?

Popping off the old tile is fairly easy—just use a heavy scraper and elbow grease. Then attack the adhesive with a razor scraper (**Photo 1**). Scrape up as much adhesive as possible, keeping the blade sharp with a sharpening stone as you go. If the adhesive is hard and brittle, use a chopping motion to break it up. Then scrape again. Even then, some of that old adhesive may be impossible to remove. If you can't get it all off, don't worry. Newer latex-modified thin-set can be applied right over the small amount that remains.

After you scrape off the adhesive, touch the floor to see if there are any sticky areas. Use a chemical adhesive remover on those parts. Find one in the flooring department at home centers.

Next locate all the cracks. You'll have to prime those areas and cover them with a peel-and-stick crack prevention mat (also called anti-fracture or crack isolation membrane; **Photo 3**) before you lay the new tile (Crack Buster Pro is one brand; a 12-in. x 25-ft. roll is $30). Skip this step and we guarantee your new tile

CAUTION: Most floor tiles made from the 1920s to the 1960s contain asbestos and require special procedures for removal. If you're unsure about yours, remove a tile and send it to a local asbestos abatement firm for testing. If it tests positive, follow these asbestos abatement procedures. Seal off the area with poly sheeting. Wear an asbestos-rated respirator. Change clothes before moving into a "clean" area. Clean the entire room with a damp cloth before removing the sheeting. Follow your local environmental codes for disposal. For more information, search the Internet for "removing asbestos tiles."

will crack right over the cracks in the concrete.

Cut the membrane so it's 1-1/2 times the width of your tiles. Then prime the concrete (see **Photo 2**) with the recommended solution (consult the membrane manufacturer's literature). Let the primer dry, and then apply the membrane (**Photos 3 and 4**).

With the cracks patched, apply a latex-modified, crack-resistant thin-set (MegaLite is one brand). Then move on to the fun part, the tile setting (see **Photo 5**). To find a dealer for Crack Buster Pro and MegaLite, go to custombuildingproducts.com (800-272-8786).

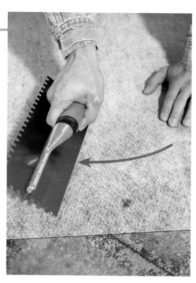

4 Push air bubbles out to the edge with a J-roller or the edge of a grout float. Then apply pressure to the entire membrane to complete the bond.

5 Force a thin layer of thin-set into the membrane fibers with the flat edge of the trowel just before combing on the thicker layer for setting the tile.

DOES NATURAL GAS REALLY DESTROY COPPER?

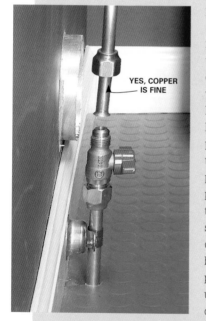

YES, COPPER IS FINE

Previously, we showed readers how to connect natural gas appliances using copper tubing. Barely a week passed before the angry letters poured in. Each was more vehement than the one before, telling us we had committed a life-threatening error by recommending copper hookups. The letters, which came from plumbers and gas company employees, maintained that natural gas should never be run in copper pipe—it must be run in steel (black pipe). They warned us that the corrosive components of natural gas can lead to leaks, explosions and, at the very least, appliance failure.

Their claims had some basis in fact 50 years ago when gas utilities drew their supplies from local wells and piped gas untreated into homes and businesses. But today, almost all natural gas in the United States and Canada is obtained from large pipeline networks. The gas in those pipelines has been treated at the wellhead or at the refinery to remove the corrosive hydrogen sulfide. This gas does NOT present a safety risk when used with copper tubing, yet the terrifying legend lives on. TFH readers should know that copper tubing is approved for gas by the National Fuel Gas Code (NFPA 54), Uniform Plumbing Code, Uniform Mechanical Code, and the International Association of Plumbing and Mechanical Officials. It has been in use in many states for more than 35 years with no safety issues.

Despite all the evidence to the contrary, some state and local building codes continue to ban the use of copper as a material for gas. Because local codes always trump national and international codes, you must obey them. Meanwhile, it's time for the 50-year-old myths and legends to die.

MOLDING
MAGIC

*Jeff Gorton reveals how to achieve
extraordinary results with ordinary moldings*

I've installed miles of trim over the years, most of it in old houses, where I've encountered every conceivable shape, size and combination of molding. I've learned a lot in the process, but I'm still discovering new tools and techniques that make trim work faster, easier and better. Here are a few tips—some classic techniques and some with a modern twist—that'll help you do a better job on your next trim project.

Combine moldings for extra drama

I love looking around old houses to see how moldings are combined to create baseboards, casings and cornices. I've even been surprised when removing old moldings to discover more layers than I originally noticed. The builders knew the advantages of combining small moldings. In addition to allowing endless possibilities for customization, smaller moldings are easier to cut and install than large moldings, and allow more flexibility on wavy or irregular walls. Plus you can often achieve a great effect for less money by combining small moldings. I made the decorative ceiling cornice shown below using moldings I found at a home center.

The best way to plan molding combinations is to get your hands on some short lengths of molding and play around with them. Many full-service lumberyards have molding samples available. At home centers, you may have to purchase short lengths of each molding you're considering, or ask for scraps.

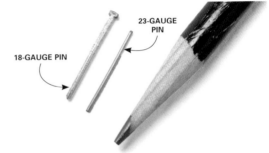

18-GAUGE PIN 23-GAUGE PIN

Nearly invisible nails

I was talking to John Frost, a local cabinetmaker, about how he installs moldings. After giving me a bunch of good tips, he said, "And of course you know about micro pinners." Actually, I didn't. John explained that a micro pinner is a finish nail gun that shoots super-thin 23-gauge pins. He uses a micro pinner because the small-diameter pins leave smaller holes that are almost invisible after you fill them. Plus the tiny pins allow him to nail very small parts without splitting them as thicker pins might.

There are several brands of micro pinners ranging in cost from $120 to $330. The more expensive models drive pins up to 2 in. long. You'll find micro pinners at home centers and online.

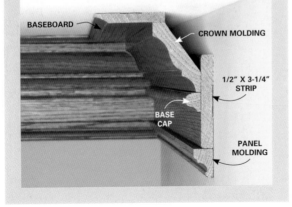

BASEBOARD CROWN MOLDING

1/2" X 3-1/4" STRIP

BASE CAP

PANEL MOLDING

23-GAUGE MICRO PINNER

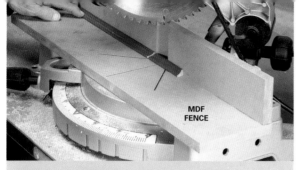

Add an auxiliary fence

I asked a cabinetmaker friend if he ever adds a fence to his miter saw, and he said, "Absolutely, always." An auxiliary fence has several advantages. It reduces the gap under and behind the molding to only what's needed for the blade to fit through. . The small gap helps prevent splintering on the back of the board and keeps small cutoffs from dropping through the fence and getting flung by the blade. You can also use the saw kerfs in the fence to help you line up your cut.

An auxiliary fence needs to be accurate but not fancy. I like to build fences from MDF because it's straight, stable and inexpensive. Another good choice is 3/4-in. plywood. Make the back of the fence as tall as possible without letting it interfere with the motor housing or blade guard. If you need several short pieces cut to the same length, make the fence long enough so you can attach a stop. Be sure the bottom and back are exactly perpendicular and that you don't put fasteners where the blade will cut. If you own a plate joiner, use glue and biscuits to join the back and bottom—no need to worry about hitting fasteners. Attach the auxiliary fence with screws through your miter saw fence.

Inspect before you buy

Moldings can vary quite a bit in looks and quality, so it pays to examine them closely when you're picking them out. It's not as critical if you're installing trim that will be painted, but for stained moldings, there are several things to watch for. Make sure moldings that will be close to each other have a similar grain pattern and that the wood is about the same tone. Chatter from shaper blades is another common problem to watch. Although you can't avoid chatter marks entirely, choosing moldings carefully can keep them to a minimum and significantly reduce your sanding time. Also watch out for "snipe," gouge cuts near the end of the molding that are caused by the molding machine. That 10-ft. stick of molding you need may not give you a full 10 ft. of usable molding.

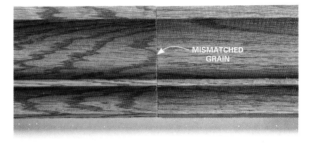

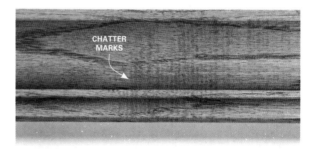

Put the pinch on miter joints

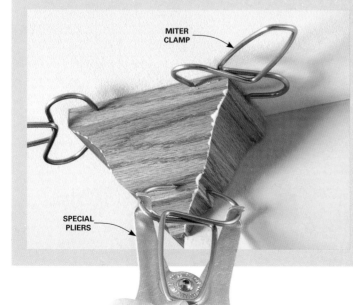

I recently ordered four miter clamps and a special pliers-type tool to install them and am amazed at how well they work. These handy little clamps are basically bent spring steel with sharp points that grab the moldings and squeeze them together. They're perfect for holding small pieces of mitered trim together while the glue dries and for clamping crown molding miters while you pin them together. They're also great for picture frame assembly. Our clamps are from Collins Tool Co. (collinstool.com; 888-838-8988; $29 for the four clamps and special pliers), but other brands are available. Search online for "miter clamps."

Spice up your project with reveals

Like every other rule, this one has many exceptions. But in general, when I'm combining moldings, or adding moldings to plain boards, I offset the parts so that the edges aren't perfectly aligned. The exposed band of molding or board is called a "reveal." Creating reveals has two big advantages. First, it allows a bit of flexibility, since the two edges don't have to be perfectly aligned. Second, reveals look better in most situations.

The typical method of creating a reveal is to set back the edge of the molding from the edge of the board as shown here. However, an equally effective method is to allow the molding to protrude. Some reveals are set by tradition. Door and window casings, for example, are usually moved about 3/16 in. from the edge of the jamb. In other cases, you'll have to trust your eye to determine the right amount.

Attach small parts with superglue

Mitered returns are tough to attach. They're usually too small to nail unless you have a micro pinner. I've tried attaching small parts with wood glue, but often the moisture from the glue causes the thinnest part of the trim to warp before the glue dries. Here's a tip I learned from a trim carpenter. Get some cyanoacrylate adhesive (CA) and activator, also known as "super glue." You may be

able to find a kit of CA that contains an activator at home centers, but a sure source is a woodworking store like Rockler. Go to rockler.com and search for "superglue" to find a wide variety. I like the medium-body CA. Spread a thin layer of CA on one piece of the molding and activator on the other. Then just press and hold for a few seconds. It works like magic, forming a strong bond unbelievably fast.

No framing— no problem

Once in a while, you may need to attach moldings where there's no framing behind the drywall to nail into. For example, if you're making frames on your wall out of moldings, it's likely that one of the vertical moldings won't have a stud behind it. The solution is to apply a thin bead of panel adhesive or construction adhesive and then tack the molding to the wall with a nail gun. For a better grip, shoot a pair of nails next to each other and at opposite angles so they form a wedge. If nails alone won't hold the molding, press it tight with 1x2s wedged against the opposite wall or the ceiling to hold it until the adhesive dries.

DIY Success Story

I built a new mantel and surround for the fireplace in my den. I decided to combine a number of different design ideas and customize it exactly as I wanted it. I used marble tile, various size pine boards and several types of molding, all from my local home center. The total cost was less than $500. FYI, I'm not a professional woodworker or builder.

—Allan Shaw

Mantel base detail

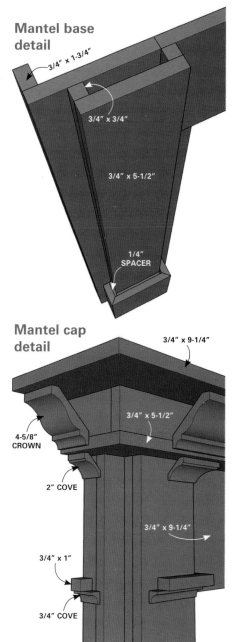

3/4" x 1-3/4"

3/4" x 3/4"

3/4" x 5-1/2"

1/4" SPACER

Mantel cap detail

3/4" x 9-1/4"

3/4" x 5-1/2"

4-5/8" CROWN

2" COVE

3/4" x 9-1/4"

3/4" x 1"

3/4" COVE

Fireplace mantel and wainscot design with SketchUp

For this article, I worked on SketchUp, a drawing program from Google, to design a fireplace mantel and simple wainscot and window trim. I used moldings that I found at a home center and a local full-service lumberyard. The SketchUp model and some of the building details are shown here. I've been dabbling in SketchUp for a few years but still have plenty to learn. What I like best about this versatile 3-D drawing program is how quickly you can learn the basics and create useful drawings. You'll be drawing 3-D shapes in minutes, and be able to draw a simple bookcase with a few hours' practice. I use SketchUp routinely to design sheds, build bookcases or just work out a tricky building detail.

Get a copy of SketchUp by going to sketchup.google.com. Then click on "Download Google SketchUp."

Wainscot detail

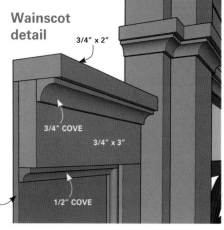

3/4" x 2"

3/4" COVE

3/4" x 3"

1/4" PLYWOOD

1/2" COVE

14 CABINET REPAIRS UNDER $14

Quick solutions to the most common cabinet problems

Some cabinet fixes are tough, even for pros. But the most common problems are easy peasy lemon squeezy, as the kindergartners like to say. Hit the hardware store in the morning to pick up supplies, then come home, get to work and you'll be done in time to feed your crew.

These fixes won't help with major problems like split panels on doors, but they will solve the little problems that bug you daily. Your cabinets will look and operate better—and sometimes a little satisfaction goes a long way.

MOUNTING SCREW
DEPTH SCREW
SIDE SCREW

1 Replace worn-out drawer slides

Lubricants won't fix damaged drawer slides. They have to be replaced. This is a common problem on silverware drawers and other drawers that carry a lot of weight. Buy new slides that are the same, or nearly the same, as your old ones. Then it's just a matter of swapping them out. You'll find a limited selection of drawer slides at home centers, but there are dozens of online sources. Three sites are drawerslides.com, thehardware-hut.com and usacabinethardware.com. These sites also sell the plastic mounting sockets that attach to the back of the cabinet to hold the slides in place.

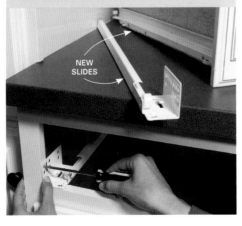

NEW SLIDES

2 Adjust Euro hinges

Adjusting cabinet doors with European hinges is as easy as turning a screw or two. Hinges like this one adjust in three directions; others adjust in two. If your door is crooked—not square with the cabinet—fix that first, then raise or lower it to the same height as adjacent doors.

For crooked doors, adjust the side screw on one hinge, which moves the door from side to side. It's a trial-and-error process. Make a small adjustment, then close the door to check its position. If the door is higher or lower than adjacent doors, loosen the mounting screws on both hinges, raise or lower the door, then tighten the screws. Place a straightedge across the door top or bottom to make sure it's level with neighboring doors.

If the door sticks out too far from the cabinet or the hinge side brushes against the cabinet when you open the door, adjust the depth screw. Some hinges move the door as you turn the depth screw; others require you to tap the door in or out and then tighten the screw.

Door adjustments aren't as easy if you have traditional hinges. If your doors are sagging, first try tightening the screws. If the hinges are bent, replace them if you can find a match.

3 Build a shelf that won't sag

Don't bother replacing a sagging shelf with another 1/2-in.-thick shelf or it'll end up sagging, too. Instead, cut a new shelf from 3/4-in. plywood. Make it the same length and 1-1/2 in. narrower (so you can add rails). Then glue and brad nail (or clamp) 1x2 rails along the front and back of the shelf, flush with the ends. The rails give the shelf additional support so it won't sag, even if you load it up with heavy cookware. Apply a polyurethane (or other) finish to match your other shelves.

3/4" PLYWOOD

1X2 LUMBER

BUMPER

4 Silence banging doors with bumpers

Doors and drawers slam loudly when wood smacks against wood. That's why most have "bumpers" near the interior corners to cushion the impact and reduce the noise. But the bumpers sometimes fall off (or kids pick them off). Get new ones at home centers ($2 for a 16-pack). Peel off the backing and stick the bumpers in place. They're available clear or with felt, and in different thicknesses. Use bumpers the same thickness as those on adjacent doors.

5 Beef up wimpy drawer bottoms

The thin plywood used for drawer bottoms sometimes gets wavy. Stiffen up the bottoms with 1/4-in. or 3/8-in. plywood. Cut the plywood to fit over the drawer bottom, leaving about a 1/4-in. gap on each side. Apply wood glue on the drawer bottom and set the plywood over it. Set a gallon or two of paint over the plywood to hold it in place until the glue dries.

6 Fill in stripped screw holes

When the screws in your hinges or drawer slides turn but don't tighten, the screw hole is stripped. That can prevent doors and drawers from closing properly. Fix the problem with glue and toothpicks. Start by removing the hardware. Then apply a drop of wood glue to the ends of toothpicks and cram as many as will fit into the hole (maybe only two or three). Wipe away any glue that drips out. Let the glue dry, then use a utility knife to cut the toothpicks flush with the cabinet or drawer. Reinstall the hardware, driving the screw through the filled hole.

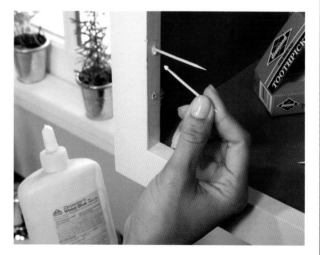

7 Repair busted drawers

Some drawers are held together by only a few drops of glue or short brad nails. When you first notice a drawer corner coming apart, take out the drawer and fix it. And if one corner is failing, others probably will, too. Save yourself future hassles by repairing all the weak corners now. Place a piece of scrap wood against a corner and lightly rap it once with a hammer. If the corner comes apart, fix it. If not, it should hold up.

To fix the corner, first remove the drawer front, if possible. Most fronts are attached by screws driven from inside the drawer. Remove any fasteners from the corner, then scrape away the old glue with a utility knife. Reglue the corner, tap the sides back together and clamp the drawer until the glue dries.

GLUE

8 Renew the shine

Grease splatters and smoke can leave a film on your cabinets, dulling the finish. Wash the cabinets with a wood cleaner to bring back the luster. Murphy Oil Soap is one type of cleaner ($4 for 32 oz.).

Use a sponge to rub the cleaner onto the cabinets. Cleaners like Murphy's don't need to be rinsed off, which cuts your cleaning time. For stubborn grease spots, scrub lightly with the cleaner using a No. 0000 steel wool pad. Cleaning the cabinets once a year keeps them shiny and protects the finish.

MAGNETIC CATCH

PLATE

9 Silence banging doors with bumpers

Sure, this trick is as old as Benny Hill jokes, but it still works. When your cabinet door is warped and won't fully close, simply install a magnetic catch (starting at $1.10 at home centers) at the problem area. Screw the magnetic catch to the cabinet rail or stile and the plate to the door. The magnet pulls the door closed. For powerful magnets, visit rockler.com and search for "magnetic catch."

10 Glue loose knobs

Once knobs fall off your cabinets, twisting them back on won't solve the problem. They'll just keep coming loose. Use a dab of thread adhesive to keep them in place (Loctite 242 is one brand; $6 at home centers). Apply the adhesive to the screw, then attach the knob. If you decide to replace the knob later, don't worry. You can remove it with a screwdriver.

THREAD ADHESIVE

11 Add back plates to cover worn areas

Years of opening doors and drawers can wear away the finish near cabinet knobs. Instead of undertaking the time-consuming task of refinishing the cabinets, try this quick fix: Install back plates under the knobs or handles. Simply unscrew the knob or handle, slide the back plate under it, then reattach the knob or handle. Back plates start at $2 and are available in a wide range of styles. You can special-order them at home centers or buy them online.

BACK PLATE

12 Replace bad latches

Older cabinets sometimes have "roller catches" that hold the doors closed. If you have these and your door won't close or stay closed, loosen the screws to slide the catch forward or backward on the cabinet frame. Or replace it if it's broken. The catches are available at home centers for less than $1.

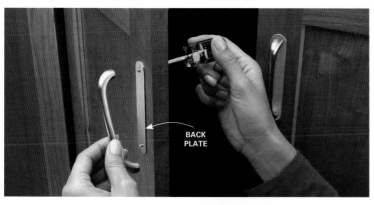

BACK PLATE

13 Fill in scratches

Use a wood fill stick ($3.50) to make scratches less visible. The stick fills in and colors over the scratch. Soften the stick with a hair dryer to make the application easier. Then run the stick over the scratch and wipe away any excess with a cloth. The fill probably won't be an exact match with the surrounding cabinet, but it'll be close. The sticks work on shallow and deep scratches. They're available at most home centers or buy them online.

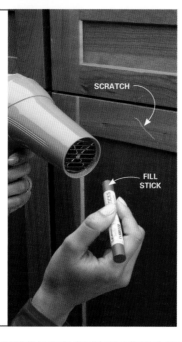

SCRATCH

FILL STICK

14 Lubricate sticking drawers

The fix for sticking drawers is easy. First remove the drawer. Wipe the drawer slides and the cabinet track with a clean cloth to remove any debris. Then spray a dry lubricant directly on the drawer slides. An 11-oz. can costs $5 at home centers; it'll say "dry lubricant" on the label. Replace the drawer and slide it in and out of the cabinet several times until it glides easily. If the drawer is still hard to open, replace the drawer slides (see p. 36).

Dry lubricants won't leave an oily residue that attracts dirt and dust. The lubricants also work great on squeaky hinges.

DIY Success Story

We replaced our sagging shelves with the white wire shelves typically used in closets. The shelves hold up well, they're inexpensive, and I can see through them—which is great when I'm searching for a specific pan, plate or coffee mug in my cabinets. You just cut the shelves to size with a hacksaw or a metal blade in a jigsaw and stick them in place.

— Maureen Riegger

DEAN'S TILE TIPS

Most pros in any trade are creatures of habit. When something works, we stick with it. But during the 15 years we've worked with Dean Sorem, our tiling consultant, he's been constantly researching his trade, trying new products and looking for a better way. So we asked Dean to show us the methods and materials he's using these days. Whether you're a tile setter or a remodeler who occasionally tackles a tile job, you're sure to find at least a few tips here that'll come in handy on your next tiling project.

Back-butter for a better bond

After returning to a floor tile job the other day to reset a loose tile, Dean decided he would make it standard procedure to back-butter every large tile he and his crew install. As bigger tiles have become more common, so has the problem of loose tiles in a finished tile job. It's harder to get a good bond with a large surface. Big tiles require a special technique: You need to trowel a thin layer of thin-set on the back of each tile before you set it. Set the loaded trowel near the center of the tile and spread a thin layer of thin-set to the edge. Then rotate the tile a quarter turn and repeat until the back is evenly covered.

BACK OF TILE

THIN-SET MORTAR

TOO SOON TO CLEAN

Don't wash the grout too soon

Dean says one of the biggest mistakes you can make on a grout job is to start cleaning up the grout too soon. Wiping the grout before it's hardened a bit allows too much water to penetrate the surface. That means blotchy-looking grout or, worse, hairline cracking and grout that falls out. To avoid these problems, be sure the grout is very firm, about like a wine cork, before you start cleaning it. Press your fingertip into the grout to test it. If it dents easily, wait.

Use a self-feeding screw gun

Screwing down backer board is monotonous and time-consuming, so when Dean discovered that cement board screws were available for self-feeding screw guns and that they didn't cost any more than loose screws, he bought a self-feeding screw gun and left his old screw gun at the shop. The Senco Duraspin tool shown is available at some home centers. If you need help locating a dealer, go to senco.com.

Corded versions of self-feeding screw guns sell for about $100 and cordless for $150. Dean actually prefers the corded version because it always offers full power and he doesn't have to worry about keeping batteries charged. With different screws, you can use the self-feeding screw gun to hang drywall or install decking, too.

COLLATED
CEMENT
BOARD
SCREWS

CHALK LINE

SELF-LEVELING
LASER LEVEL

Plan layouts with a laser level

Laser levels save time and increase accuracy. Dean uses a self-leveling laser to help plan the tile layout. He projects a level line around the room and measures from it to determine the size of the cut tiles along the edges. Then, after figuring out an ideal layout, he uses the laser as a guide to chalk layout lines. The laser saves time by eliminating the fussy job of extending level lines around the room with a 4-ft. level.

Dean uses the Stanley FatMax Cross Line Laser (about $100), which is self-leveling and projects level and plumb lines. Self-leveling lasers reduce setup time and can be swiveled without readjustment. Mount the laser on an inexpensive ($25) camera tripod for maximum versatility. More-expensive lasers project perpendicular lines on the floor that you can use to plan floor layouts.

WATERPROOFING MEMBRANE

SHOWER TRAY

DRAIN

CURB

Use a Schluter system for a leakproof shower

Dean loves the simplicity and security offered by the Schluter shower system. Before, he had to pour a sloped mortar bed, cover it with a waterproof membrane and then pour another layer of mortar over that. This traditional method is tricky and time-consuming, and the shower will leak if it's not perfectly executed.

The Schluter system eliminates all these hassles by providing the tile setter with a preformed shower base and curb, a special drain and a waterproofing membrane. Schluter even includes preformed inside and outside corner pieces to seal these tricky spots. All you need to provide is unmodified thin-set and some tools.

The complete system for a 48-in. square shower costs about $400. Dean likes feeling confident that his showers won't leak and being able to start tiling right away without waiting for mortar to set up. For information on where to buy the Schluter system and how to install it, go to schluter.com (800-472-4588).

Instructions are included with the kit, but here's an overview. You embed the foam base and curb in thin-set. Then you install the special drain assembly, embedding it in thin-set as you attach it to the drainpipe. Finally, you'll embed the waterproof membrane in a layer of unmodified thin-set and tile over it. The membrane and corner pieces can be installed in any order.

Polish stone edges

To save money and get a better-looking job, Dean prefers to make his own trim pieces for marble, granite and other stone tile jobs. Take the top of a shower curb, for example. You would have to buy enough bullnose trim to cover both edges, and you'd end up with a grout joint down the center where the two rows of bullnose meet. Dean covers the curb with one piece of stone, polished on both edges.

Dean prefers the honeycomb-style dry diamond polishing pads with hook-and-loop fasteners. They allow him to quickly run through a series of grits from 60 to 800 or higher without wasting a lot of time changing pads. One caveat, though. This type of disc requires a variable-speed grinder because the maximum allowable rpm is about 4,000. If you own a single-speed grinder that runs at 10,000 rpm, you'll need a set of PVA Marble Edge Polisher discs that are safe to run at high speed (they polish all kinds of stone). One source for both types of discs is Benfer Blade & Saw (benfertool.com; 952-888-1448), or search online for "marble polishing discs."

Polishing stone is a dusty operation, so work outside. Start by using the coarsest grit to remove the saw marks from all the edges. Then progress through the grits until you reach the level of sheen you desire. Use light pressure to avoid overheating the disc and wearing it out prematurely. You'll have to progress through the finest grit to create a glossy surface.

BOTH EDGES POLISHED

Waterproof wet areas

It's a surprise to most people that a tiled wall or floor isn't waterproof. Some types of tile are porous, and most grout isn't waterproof either. Water can seep through tile and grout and leak into cracks at corners and other intersections. The only sure way to keep water from reaching the backer board is to waterproof all areas that may be exposed to water. That's easy with the new waterproofing coatings. Dean uses the RedGuard brand, but there are others. Dean says, "If in doubt, coat it with waterproofing."

Follow the application instructions on the container. Dean applies the RedGuard with an inexpensive paint pad, which he prefers to a brush or roller because it works like a trowel, allowing him to quickly spread a thick, even layer over the surface.

RED GUARD

PAINT PAD APPLICATOR

Flatten walls with shims

Modern tile backer board beats a traditional mortar bed—unless you're trying to flatten a crooked wall. In the old days, a skillful tile setter could float mortar over the waviest framing and end up with a perfectly flat surface. Nowadays most tilers use some type of tile backer board. But if you screw backer boards to crooked framing, you'll get a wavy surface that makes it tough to do a nice tile job.

The solution is to flatten the walls before you screw the board to them. Dean chooses the longest level or straight screed board that will fit across a wall and uses it to see if any studs are bowed in or out. If a stud is really bowed out (1/4 in. or more) Dean saws a kerf about two-thirds through the stud at its midpoint and pushes it back. Then he'll screw a straight stud alongside to hold it in place. In most cases, though, shimming the studs with thin strips of cardboard to get them into alignment is enough. You can buy long, thin strips of cardboard for shimming at some home centers, but any strips of thin material will work. Leftover vinyl flooring cut into 1-1/2-in. strips is a good alternative.

THIN CARDBOARD SHIM

TRIPLE YOUR CLOSET SPACE

FOR ANY SIZE CLOSET!

If you have to dig through a mountain of clothes to find your favorite sweatshirt, it's time to take on that messy closet. This simple-to-build system organizes your closet with shelf, drawer and hanging space for your clothes, shoes and accessories. Buying a closet system like this would cost you at least $500, but you can build this one for about half that.

Our system is really just four plywood boxes outfitted with shelf standards, closet rods or drawers. We built it for an 8-ft.-wide closet with an 8-ft. ceiling, but it'll work in any reach-in closet that's at least 6 ft. wide if you adjust the shelf width between the boxes or change the box dimensions.

Three times the storage—and more!

Three times the storage in the same space may sound impossible, but just look at the numbers:

STORAGE SPACE COMPARISON FOR 8-FT. CLOSET

before ■ after ■

	before	after
SHELVES	8 FT.	28 FT.
DRAWERS	0	4
CLOTHES ROD	8 FT.	8 FT.
BASKET	0	1
HIS STUFF		
HER STUFF		

Time, money and materials

You can complete this project in a weekend. Spend Saturday cutting the lumber, ironing on the edge banding and applying the finish. Use your Saturday date night to clean everything out of the closet. That leaves you Sunday to build and install the new system.

We built the entire system with birch plywood ($40 per sheet). The total cost, including the hardware for the drawers, shelves and closet rods, was about $250 (see Shopping List, p. 49). You could use MDF ($30) or oak plywood ($40) instead of birch. Everything you need for this project is available at home centers.

Cut and prefinish the parts

Start by cutting all the parts to size following **Figure C** on p. 49 and the Cutting List on p. 46. The corner box sides are slightly narrower than 12 in., so you can cut off dings and dents and still cut four sides from a sheet of plywood.

You won't be able to cut the shelves that fit between the boxes to length until the boxes are installed (the shelves need to be cut to fit), but you can rip plywood to 11-7/8 in. and cut the shelves to length later.

Once the parts are cut, apply edge banding (iron-on veneer) to all the edges that will be exposed after the boxes are assembled (**Figure A**). Build a jig to hold the parts upright. Place a part in the jig. Then cut the edge banding so it overhangs each end of the plywood by 1/2 in. Run an

1 Finish now, save time later. Prefinishing gives you a faster, neater finish because you'll have fewer corners to mess with. Apply two coats of polyurethane quickly and smoothly with a disposable paint pad.

PAINT PAD

2 Preinstall drawer slides. Attaching slides is a lot easier before the boxes are assembled. Position the slides using reference lines and a spacer. Remember that there are left- and right-hand slides, usually marked "CL" and "CR."

SPACER

REFERENCE

3 Gang-cut the standards. Cutting 16 standards one by one with a hacksaw would take hours. Instead, bundle two or more together with tape and cut them with a jigsaw.

SHELF STANDARDS

METAL BLADE

DIY Success Story

"Years ago, I built a closet storage system. I made two mistakes. First, I didn't have enough drawers. You can never have too many drawers. But my biggest mistake was using cheap plastic holders for the closet rods. When the first one broke and dumped heaps of clothing on the floor—which had to be ironed again—I bit the bullet and replaced them all. I used the beefy, more expensive metal holders—I could hang suits of armor on them and they wouldn't break."

— Mike O'Brien

Figure A
Closet storage system

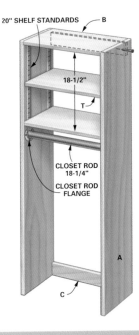

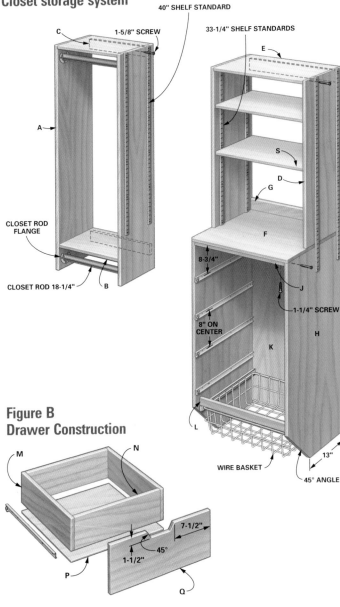

Figure B
Drawer Construction

iron (on the cotton setting) slowly over the edge banding. Then press a scrap piece of wood over the edge banding to make sure it's fully adhered. Trim the edges with a veneer edge trimmer ($10).

Lightly sand the wood and your closet rod with 120-grit sandpaper. Wipe away the dust with a tack cloth, then use a paint pad to apply a coat of polyurethane ($6 per half pint) on everything except the drawer parts (**Photo 1**). This $2 pad will let you finish each part in about 20 seconds. Let the finish dry, then apply a second coat.

Attach the hardware

It's easier to install the drawer slides and the shelf standards that go inside the boxes before you assemble the boxes. Use a framing square to draw reference lines on the drawer unit sides for your drawer slides

CUTTING LIST		
KEY	QTY.	SIZE & DESCRIPTION
A	4	3/4" x 11-7/8" x 52" corner box sides
B	4	3/4" x 11-7/8" x 18-1/2" corner box tops and bottom
C	4	3/4" x 2-1/2" x 18-1/2" corner box screw strips
D	2	3/4" x 13-7/8" x 34" shelf unit sides
E	1	3/4" x 13-7/8" x 22-1/2" shelf unit top
F	1	3/4" x 21" x 24" shelf unit bottom
G	2	3/4" x 2-1/2" x 22-1/2" shelf unit screw strips
H	2	3/4" x 20-3/4" x 44" drawer unit sides
J	1	3/4" x 20-3/4" x 22-1/2" drawer unit top
K	1	1/4" x 24" x 44" drawer unit back
L	1	3/4" x 2" x 22-1/2" drawer unit cleat
M	8	1/2" x 6" x 20" drawer sides
N	8	1/2" x 6" x 20" drawer fronts and backs
P	4	1/4" x 20" x 19" drawer bottoms
Q	4	3/4" x 7-3/4" x 22-1/4" drawer face
R	8	3/4" x 11-7/8" adjustable shelves, cut to length (not shown)
S	2	3/4" x 13-7/8" x 22" adjustable shelves for shelf unit
T	1	3/4" x 11-7/8" x 18" right corner box adjustable shelf
U	1	3/4" x 14-1/4" x 96" top shelf (not shown)

(see **Figure A**). The slides are spaced 8 in. apart, centered 8-3/4 in. down from the top of the box. Keep the slides 3/4 in. from the front edge (this is where the drawer faces will go). Use a 7/64-in. self-centering drill bit ($9) to drill pilot holes and screw the slides into place (**Photo 2**).

You'll need to have your wire basket now (they're available at home centers). Attach the glides for the basket 3 in. below the drawer slides. If your basket is narrower than 22-1/2 in., screw a cleat to the box side so the basket will fit.

Now attach the shelf standards. You can cut them with a hacksaw, but an easier way is to use a metal blade in a jigsaw. Place two or more standards together so the numbers are oriented the same way and the standards are aligned at the ends. Tape the standards together where you're going to make the cut, then gang-cut them with your jigsaw (**Photo 3**).

Screw the standards to the inside of the box sides, 1 in. from the edges. Keep the standards 3/4 in. from the top (that's where the box tops go). Be sure the numbers on the standards are facing the same way when you install them—this ensures the shelves will be level.

Assemble the boxes

Use a brad nailer to tack the boxes together following **Figure A** and **Photo 4**. If you don't have a brad nailer, use clamps. Then screw the boxes together. We used 1-5/8-in. trim screws ($5 for a 1-lb. box) because the screw heads are small and unobtrusive (we left the screw heads exposed). Here are some tips for assembling the boxes:

- Attach the screw strips to the box tops first, then add one side, then the bottom shelf, and then the second side.
- Drill 1/8-in. pilot holes to prevent splitting. Stay 1 in. from edges.
- If your cuts are slightly off and the top, bottom and sides aren't exactly the same width, align the front edges.
- The boxes will be slightly wobbly until they're installed in the closet, so handle them with care.

4 **Nail first, then screw. If you have a brad nailer, tack the boxes together to hold the parts in position. Then add screws for strength.**

GLUE

FRAMING SQUARE

SPACER

5 **Square the drawer boxes. If the boxes aren't square, the drawers won't fit right or glide smoothly. Drawers take a beating, so assemble them with nails and glue.**

DOUBLE-SIDED TAPE

6 **Center the drawer faces perfectly. Stick the faces to the boxes with double-sided tape. Then pull out the drawer and drive screws from inside the box.**

- The middle bottom box has a back. Square the box with the back, then glue and tack the back in place.
- After the corner boxes are assembled, screw shelf standards to the side that doesn't abut the wall (it's easier to install the standards before the boxes are installed).

Build the drawers

Cut the drawer sides and bottoms (see Cutting List, p. 46). Assemble the sides with glue and 1-in. screws. To square the drawers, set adjacent sides against a framing square that's clamped to your work surface. Glue and tack the drawer bottom into place (**Photo 5**). Then set the drawer slides on the drawers, drill pilot holes and screw the slides into place.

Install the drawers in the box. Getting the drawer faces in their perfect position is tricky business. If the faces are even slightly off-center, the drawer won't close properly. To align them, place double-sided tape over the drawer front. Starting with the top drawer, center the drawer face in the opening (**Photo 6**). You should have about a 1/8-in. gap on both sides and the top. Press the face into the tape. Take out the drawer and clamp the face to the drawer to keep it stationary. Drive two 1-in. screws through the inside of the drawer into the face.

Hang the boxes in the closet

Now install the boxes. Start by drawing a level line in the closet, 11 in. down from the ceiling. This will give you just over 10 in. of storage space above the closet system after the top shelf is installed. Then mark the stud locations on the wall with tape.

Don't assume your closet walls are plumb—they're probably not. So you can't just place a box in a corner without checking for alignment. Hanging the boxes is a two-person job, so get a helper. Start with the

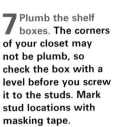

7 Plumb the shelf boxes. **The corners of your closet may not be plumb, so check the box with a level before you screw it to the studs. Mark stud locations with masking tape.**

8 Install the center unit in two parts. **The center unit is big and clumsy, so install the shelf unit first, then prop up the drawer unit with spacers and screw it to the shelf.**

corner boxes. Align the top of the box with your level line on the wall. Have your helper plumb the box with a level while you drive 2-1/2-in. screws through the screw strip into the wall at the stud locations (**Photo 7**). Attach the other corner box the same way.

Find the center of the wall, then make a mark 12 in. on one side of the center mark. That's where your shelf unit will go. Again, have your helper plumb the box while you align it with your marks and screw it to the wall.

Prop up the drawer unit on spacers so it's tight against the shelf unit. Align the edges, then clamp the boxes and screw them together

(**Photo 8**). Drive screws through the screw strip into the wall.

Then place the top shelf over the boxes. We could just barely fit our shelf into the closet to lift it into place. If yours won't fit, you'll have to cut it and install it as two pieces. Make the cut near one end, over a corner box, so it's not noticeable. Screw the shelf to the box tops with 1-1/4-in. screws.

Then attach shelf standards along the sides of the shelf and drawer units (**Figure A**). Cut the adjustable shelves to length to fit between the corner boxes and the middle boxes. Finally, screw the closet rod flanges into place, cut the closet rod to size and install the rods.

Figure C
Closet storage cutting diagrams

We're showing only the 3/4-in. plywood here. The 1/2-in. and 1/4-in. plywood sheets are for the drawers and back.

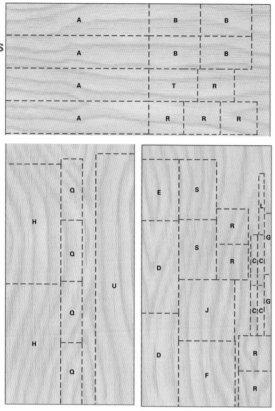

SHOPPING LIST

ITEM	QTY.
4' x 8' x 3/4" plywood	3
4' x 8' x 1/2" plywood	1
4' x 8' x 1/4" plywood	1
8' closet rod	1
Edge banding (iron-on veneer)	2 pkgs.
20" drawer slides	4 prs.
6' shelf standards	10
Closet rod flanges	10
Wire basket	1
2-1/2" screws	1 box
1-5/8" trim screws	1 box
1-1/4" screws	1 box
1" screws	1 box
Wipe-on poly	1 pint

Handy Hints®

"Hot" vinyl tile removal tip

Here's a hot tip for removing a damaged vinyl tile that needs replacement. Put a cloth down on the tile and hold an iron set on medium- high on it for about 10 seconds. The cloth keeps the tile from melting but makes it pliable and softens the adhesive backing. Tease a corner free with the tip of a utility knife and the tile will peel right up. This works with both peel-and-stick and glue-down tiles.

DAMAGED TILE

Stay-put insulation

I was insulating the vaulted ceiling in our new bedroom, and I couldn't get the unfaced fiberglass batts to stay put long enough to staple up the plastic moisture barrier. Then I spied a roll of paper drywall tape. Yes! I stapled it across the bottom of the rafters as I pushed the batts into place. It was easy to go back and fluff the batts against the rafters before I stapled up the plastic.

I ♥ KITCHEN ROLLOUTS

*They changed editor Elisa Bernick's life—
and they'll change yours, too!*

It may sound like hype, but adding rollouts to your kitchen cabinets can be life-changing. I speak from personal experience. I recently added rollouts to our entire kitchen, and this is what happened:

- The kids have complete access to everything they need—from cereal to the recycling. Now they can get their own breakfast and take the cans to the curb—no excuses!
- My sore back and my husband's bum knee are less of an issue since we no longer have to constantly stoop to find things in our base cabinets.
- Dinner prep goes a lot faster now that we're not hunting for pot lids and baking pans piled on top of one another on our jumbled, dark shelves.
- We're saving money by not buying things we already have (but that had been lost in the recesses of our cabinets). We can pull our shelves into the light and see everything, including the rancid oil and three boxes of cornstarch we somehow acquired—need some?
- The kitchen feels larger and works better. The rollouts maximize every cubic inch of storage space, so I can store rarely used appliances in my cabinets instead of on my counters.

Are you a convert yet? This article will give you tips for planning, buying and building kitchen rollouts so they can change your life too. You can build a simple rollout drawer like the ones shown here, in a couple of hours for $20. But don't say I didn't warn you. Once you see that rollout in action, you'll want to retrofit all your kitchen cabinets. What are you waiting for?

Make the most of skinny spaces

Kitchen designer Mary Jane Pappas typically recommends 18- to 30-in.-wide rollout drawers for cabinets: "Any larger and they're too clumsy. Any smaller and too much of the space is used by the rollouts themselves." But there is one type of rollout that makes good use of narrow spaces, even those only 3 to 6 in. wide. Pappas says that pullout pantries—single tall, narrow drawers with long, shelves, drawers, baskets or even Peg-Board (photo at right)—can be an efficient way to put skinny spaces to work.

In a small kitchen with little storage space, you can make even narrow filler spaces work harder by installing a vertical pegboard rollout. Shown is the 434 Series 6-in. Base Filler with stainless steel panel, $315, from Rev-A-Shelf.com.

REV-A-SHELF

Make drawer boxes about 1/32 in. smaller than you need. It's easy to shim behind a slide with layers of masking tape to make up for a too-small drawer. It's a lot harder to deal with a drawer that's too wide.

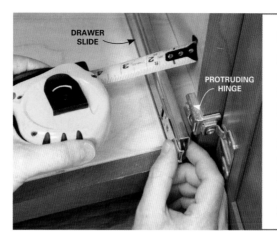

Watch for obstacles

Every cabinetmaker has a story about the rollout that wouldn't roll out but instead collided with something. When you're measuring for the spacer width, watch out for protruding hinges and doors that don't open fully or that protrude into the cabinet opening.

Baltic birch is best

Cabinetmakers love Baltic birch plywood for rollouts because the edges look great. Unlike standard hardwood plywood, Baltic birch never has voids in the inner core. It may not be labeled "Baltic birch" at home centers, but you'll be able to identify it by comparing it with other hardwood plywood in the racks. It'll have more and thinner laminations in the plywood core. The biggest disadvantages of using Baltic birch are that it costs more than standard hardwood plywood and can be harder to find. A 4 x 8-ft. sheet will run you $65 compared with $50 for standard hardwood plywood. If your home center doesn't carry it, try a traditional lumberyard.

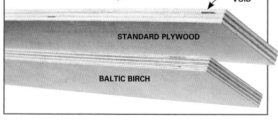

STANDARD PLYWOOD

BALTIC BIRCH

VOID

Start at the bottom

The most useful rollout shelves and drawers are the ones closest to the floor since these eliminate the most awkward bending and crouching. If you want to limit your time and money investment, you'll get the most bang for your buck by retrofitting these areas first.

Use the right slides

There are a dozen kinds of drawer slides out there, but if you want to keep shopping and installation simple, stick to these two types:

Roller slides glide on plastic wheels. They're inexpensive, a cinch to install (it takes about two minutes) and nearly impossible to screw up. You'll find them at home centers under various names including side mount, under mount and bottom mount. Most are rated to carry 35 to 100 lbs. For heavy-duty rollouts holding items such as canned goods, use slides rated for at least 100 lbs. The big disadvantage: Most roller slides extend only three-quarters of their length—the back of the drawer stays in the cabinet.

Ball-bearing slides glide on tiny bearings. The big advantage of these slides is that they extend fully, giving you complete access to everything in the drawer.

They're about three times the cost of roller slides, and they're usually rated to carry 75 to 100 lbs., but you can get 200-lb. versions for about $40 a pair. Home centers carry ball-bearing slides, but you'll find a wider variety at woodworkershardware.com. The big disadvantage: They're fussy to install. If your drawer is a hair too big or small, these slides won't glide.

FULL-EXTENSION SLIDE

THREE-QUARTERS SLIDE

Roller slides are inexpensive and easy to install, but they only extend three-quarters.

Ball-bearing slides cost more and are harder to install, but they can extend fully.

Think inside the box

Building a slew of identical drawer boxes is easier, but having a variety gives you more versatility. Think about what you're going to store and build the boxes to suit your needs.

Rollout drawers with sloping sides keep tall things stable yet still let you see all the way to the back of the shelf. These are good for nesting pots and pans or storing different-size items on the same shelf.

Lower sides (3 in. is typical) work well for smaller items such as canned goods and spices. The low sides make reading labels easier.

Shelves with higher sides all around (6 in. tall rather than the typical 3 in.) are ideal for tippy plastic storage containers or stacks of plates.

Store-bought rollouts—what to look for

You can spend as little as $10 for a simple wire rollout basket or as much as $100. So what's the difference?

- Look for rollouts with quality hardware. Second-rate slides and rollers can sag or seize up under sacks of flour and pots and pans. Examine the slides to check whether they're roller slides (which extend only three-quarters of their length) or ball-bearing (which extend fully). Ball-bearing slides tend to support heavier items and roll more smoothly.

IKEA's Rationell Variera pullout basket ($20; ikea.com) works well for medium-weight items.

- Choose sturdy, chrome-plated steel rollouts for heavier items. Steel rollouts come in different gauge metals. Before ordering online, shop around at different retailers so you can physically compare the weight and density of the steel used by different manufacturers.

The Lynk Rollout Undersink Drawer ($65 at home centers) can take heavy use.

- Epoxy-coated wire rollouts and plastic inserts work fine for light-duty items, but they have a tendency to crack, bend and scratch if packed with heavy loads like canned goods.

Rubbermaid's Slide Out Undersink Basket (No. 80360; $20 at home centers) handles light items.

Avoid mistakes with a story stick

The most obvious way to size rollout parts is to measure the opening of the cabinet and then do the math. But that's a recipe for mistakes because it's easy to forget to subtract one of the components (like the width of the slides or the drawers) from the overall measurement. So try this: Forget the math and mark your measurements on a piece of scrap wood. It's a great visual aid that helps you prevent mistakes and having to walk between your kitchen and your shop constantly to double-check measurements.

Mark the exact widths of your rollout parts on a stick. That eliminates the math—and the mistakes.

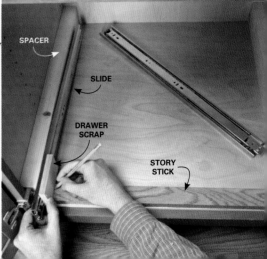

SPACER

SLIDE

DRAWER SCRAP

STORY STICK

Divide up wide spaces

If the cabinet is more than 30 in. wide, consider installing two narrower rollouts side by side rather than a single wide one. This means some extra building work and buying more slides, but the smaller rollouts will operate more smoothly and easily. Wider shelves and drawers tend to bind or rack as you slide them in and out.

DIVIDER

READER PHOTO

Reader Success Story

"My daughter called her pantry "the black hole" because she could never find what she needed on the deep shelves. I replaced the five full-width shelves with two six-drawer stacks of sturdy full-extension drawers from IKEA, supported by interior center panels. We spaced the drawers carefully for the types of items she planned to store. Finishing touches include soft-close dampers on the drawers and iron-on edge-banding for the birch plywood panels." [The Rationell 18-in.-deep, fully extending drawers cost about $38 each at ikea.com.]

— Jim Wagener

Confessions of a rollaholic

I'm addicted to rollouts. Last winter I replaced every single cabinet shelf in our kitchen with rollouts, custom-designed for whatever needed storing. I've built about 15 more for my shop. I've learned that the key to a useful rollout is to decide what you want it to hold and design it around that purpose. These vertical rollouts in my shop are dedicated to jugs, cans and jars of finishes and solvents. Before starting, I carefully laid out exactly what would go on each shelf on the workbench to get the sizes and spacing just right. They work fantastic.

Travis Larson (aka Shop Rat)

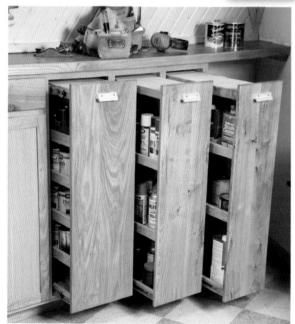

Keep drawer boxes simple

All the drawer boxes in my shop are super simple: butt-joint corners and glued-on bottoms. No rabbets, dadoes or dovetails. They don't look very impressive, but they've held up for years. So I built my kitchen rollouts the same way. If simple boxes can carry tools and hardware, I figure they can stand up to kitchen use, too.

—*Gary Wentz, Senior Editor*

Field editor tip:
Consider having drawer boxes made to your exact specs and then install them yourself. The average cost of a solid maple, dovetailed single drawer that we order is about $35. Compared with buying material and finishing it yourself—not to mention the dovetail joints—you can't beat it. And it looks much nicer.

—*Steve Zubik, Nest Woodworking, Northfield, MN*

ROLLOUTS GALORE!

Get ideas, inspiration and plans on our new Web site!
Be sure to visit familyhandyman.com and search "kitchen storage."

Simple pantry rollouts

A great way to get more storage space in even the smallest kitchen is by putting those narrow spaces and filler areas to work with a rollout pantry. We have two great projects to choose from. One is a handle-free version that lets you line up more than one rollout bin in a single cabinet. The other is a more traditional, three-drawer pantry rollout that reuses your existing cabinet door and hardware. Both versions make it possible for you to use every cubic inch of storage space in your kitchen.

Rollouts for underused locations

The space under sinks is often overlooked, but it's prime real estate for rollouts. This article gives step-by-step instructions for how to build two types of customizable rollout trays that fit around and below plumbing pipes, garbage disposers and other obstacles beneath your sink. These rollouts transform that "I'm not sure what's under there" storage space into an organized and efficient location for cleaning supplies that lets you see everything you've got in one glance.

Classic rollout shelves plus a trash center

Base cabinets have the least convenient storage in your kitchen. This article will show you how to bring everything in your cabinets within easy reach by retrofitting your base cabinets with classic rollout shelves. It also shows how to construct a special rollout for recycling and trash without using expensive bottom-mount hardware. The article gives you step-by-step instructions for measuring, building the rollout drawer and its carrier, attaching the drawer slides, and mounting the unit in the cabinet.

Rollouts at ankle level

Turn wasted toe-kick cavities into clever flat storage space for serving trays, cutting boards and baking pans. This article shows you how to construct self-contained rollout shelving units that you assemble in your shop and then just slip into place beneath your existing cabinets. The article steps you through measuring and building the shelf and carrier units, and then installing them in your kitchen. Even if you've never built or installed a drawer before, this article will show you how.

BILL ZUEHLKE (4)

PRO **TILE TIPS**

Specal tricks for special tile

LAYOUT
LINE →

Build a pyramid for diagonal layouts

The usual way to lay tile diagonally is to mark 45-degree diagonal lines on the wall or floor. But when that angle isn't 45 degrees, as with the diamond-shaped tile you see here, getting exact lines is even harder. So we'll show you a better way: Mark a single layout line and center the tiles over it by aligning the corners of the tile with the line. Build a pyramid centered on the line and use the sides of the pyramid to align each diagonal course. Check the sides of the pyramid occasionally with a straightedge.

Nobody knows tile like our guru, Dean Sorem. Over the past 25 years, he's covered thousands of walls and floors with tile of every type. Based in Hudson, WI, Dean is the head honcho of Sorem Tile and Stone (soremtile.com).

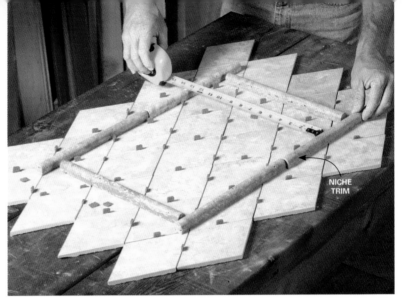

NICHE TRIM

Size a niche to suit the tile

If you're planning a wall niche, lay out the tile and take some measurements to determine the size of the niche. If you custom-size the niche to fit between full tiles, you'll get a better-looking installation and avoid some cutting. With a diagonal tile layout like the one shown here, you'll get full tiles and half tiles. If trim will frame the niche, be sure to factor it into the layout.

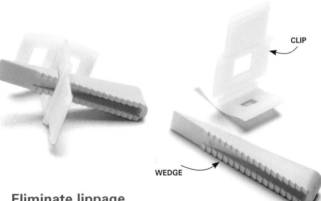

CLIP

WEDGE

Eliminate lippage

"Lippage" is the technical term for uneven tile edges. Lippage is hard to avoid with large tile and easy to see with narrow grout lines or tile that has square—rather than rounded—edges. In any of those circumstances, leveling clips and wedges help you lay tile flat. Just slip the clip under the tile and push in the wedge. After the thin-set

hardens, break off the exposed clip. LASH brand clips are available at most home centers ($20 for 96 clips and wedges) or shop online at qep.com.

Special mortar for big tiles

Thin-set mortar is the best bedding adhesive for most tile. But if you're setting tiles larger than 12 x 12 in., look for terms like "medium bed," "large tile" or "large format" on the bag label. Bigger tile requires a thicker bed, and unlike standard thin-set, medium-bed mortar doesn't lose its bonding strength when you lay it on thick. It's also firmer and shrinks less, so tiles stay in position better while the mortar hardens. Medium-bed mortar is available at tile stores and some home centers.

Clean cuts in porcelain

Porcelain tile is incredibly hard—and incredibly brittle. So it often chips along cuts or cracks before the cut is complete. Here's a three-step routine that eliminates those problems. The first step only works with saws that allow you to adjust the depth of cut. If yours doesn't, you can still make the second and third cuts to avoid cracks.

1 Score. **Make a shallow cut across the tile—about 1/8 in. deep. This minimizes chipping.**

2 Slit. **Cut a finishing end slit about 2 in. long. This prevents cracking as you approach the end of the main cut.**

3 Slice. **Make the main cut as usual. Don't rush it; slow, steady pressure creates the cleanest cut.**

Don't trust this chart

Your thin-set probably has a chart like this on the label. Don't rely on it. The recommendations are a good starting point, but they don't guarantee a thin-set bed thick enough to provide full contact with the tile. And without full contact, you don't get full support or adhesion.

As the chart shows, larger tiles require larger trowel notches (to provide a thicker bed). But other factors matter too: the flatness of the wall or floor, or the texture of the tile's back. So the only reliable way to know that the bed is thick enough is to set the first few tiles, then immediately pry them up. If the tile hasn't made full contact, you'll see it. The easiest solution is to use the next notch size. With

AVERAGE COVERAGE / COBERTURA PROMEDIO		
TILE SIZE TAMAÑO DE AZUELOS Y BALDOSAS	TROWEL SIZE TAMAÑO DE LLANA	PER 25 LB BAG POR BOLSA DE 11.34 KG
Up to 8" Hasta 20 cm	1/4" x 1/4" x 1/4" Square-Notch 6 x 6 x 6 mm Dentada Cuadrada	45 - 50 sq. ft. 4.2 - 4.6 m²
8" to 12" 20 a 30 cm	1/4" x 3/8" x 1/4" Square-Notch 6 x 9 x 6 mm Dentada Cuadrada	32 - 35 sq. ft. 2.9 - 3.3 m²
12" or larger 30 cm o más	1/2" x 1/2" x 1/2" Square-Notch 13 x 13 x 13 mm Dentada Cuadrada	23 - 25 sq. ft. 2.1 - 2.3 m²

tiles larger than 12 in., it's a good idea to also "back butter" them with thin-set. Also keep an eye on "squeeze-out" during the job. If you don't see thin-set squeezing out between tiles, pull up a tile to check coverage.

Big cuts without a big saw

Huge tiles are popular these days, and the best way to cut them is with a big, expensive tile saw. Here's the next best way: a handheld wet saw guided by a straight-edge (we used a plywood scrap). The Ryobi TC400 saw shown ($90), along with the three-step cutting method shown on p. 57, gave us perfectly straight cuts in porcelain tile (but with some chipping). A cement-mixing tub ($10) caught most of the mess.

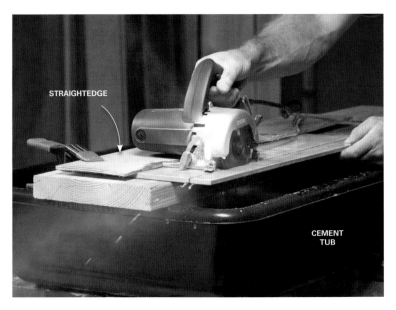

STRAIGHTEDGE

CEMENT TUB

Get a handle on tile

A suction cup ($10) lets you lift a sunken tile or adjust a crooked one. Some home centers and hardware stores carry them; most don't. To shop online, search for "suction cup handle." Keep in mind that they only work on smooth-faced tile.

Gentle smudge remover

When you're shopping for tile supplies, take a detour to the sandpaper aisle and pick up a pack of fine abrasive pads ($2). Along with a little water, they're great for removing stubborn thin-set smudges on the face of tile. And they won't scratch the glossy glaze.

Absolutely essential trowel

Tile setters use a margin trowel for everything: prying up sunken tiles, nudging crooked ones, cleaning out grout lines, mixing up small batches of thin-set or grout, scooping mix out of the bucket and scraping up messes. Makes a great back scratcher, too. If you're setting tile, you've got to have one ($6 at home centers).

Tools&Skills

NEW-AGE **DRYWALL CORNER BEAD**

Traditional metal corner bead is tedious and time consuming to install, and if you don't cover it with tape, it's likely to develop cracks along the edges. Luckily there's an alternative that's simpler to install and won't crack. If you're an old-school carpenter like me, you've probably dismissed paper-faced corner bead as an inferior DIY product, but trust me, once you try it, you'll never go back.

You'll find paper-faced corner bead alongside standard metal corners in home centers and drywall supply stores.

It costs a little more, about $3 for an 8-ft. length versus $2 for metal bead. But it's worth every penny.

Pros use a special hopper to apply joint compound to the corner bead and an expensive rolling tool to embed the bead, but you can get the same benefits using a 3-in. stiff putty knife, a 5- or 6-in. flexible putty knife and a spray bottle filled with water. Here's how to install paper-faced corner bead, including a few tips to simplify the job and avoid problems.

PAPER FACE

METAL INSIDE

1 Cut it with tin snips. If you need to cut pieces to length, simply hold the bead in place, mark the cut, and cut the bead with tin snips. Where pieces run to the floor, cut them about 1/2 in. short. The baseboard will cover the gap.

3 Mist the bead. Wetting the paper covering on the corner bead helps create a better bond and better adhesion and cuts down on wrinkles. Do this by spritzing the corner bead before you stick it to the wall. You don't have to soak the corner bead; just dampen it a bit.

6" PUTTY KNIFE

2 Mud the corner. Spread a thick layer of all-purpose joint compound on both sides of the corner and smooth it off with a putty knife. Avoid lightweight joint compound because it doesn't adhere as well to the corner bead. Strive for an even, consistent layer of joint compound about 1/8 in. thick. Don't leave any thin or dry spots.

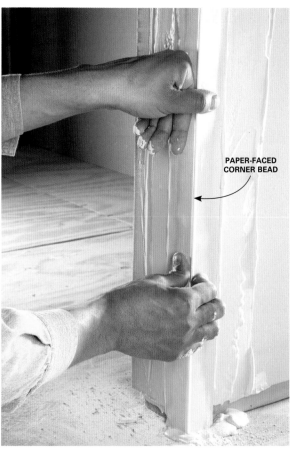

PAPER-FACED CORNER BEAD

4 Position the bead. Press the dampened corner bead into the joint compound with your fingers. Run your fingers up and down while pressing evenly on both sides to embed and center the corner bead.

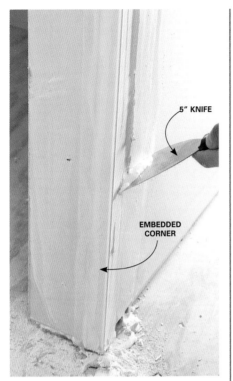

5" KNIFE

EMBEDDED CORNER

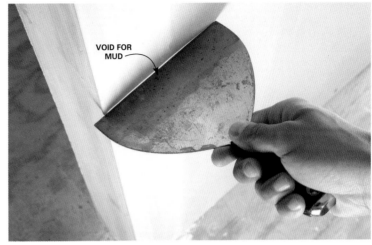

VOID FOR MUD

7 Check the corner with your blade. **A perfectly positioned corner bead protrudes slightly at the corner to allow a void for joint compound.** After you place the bead, check for a void by setting your 6-in. putty knife against the corner to make sure there's a space under it. Check both sides in several places along the length of the corner. Slide the corner in or out to make adjustments. Use staples to hold the corner in place if it won't stay put.

5 Embed the tape. **After positioning the bead, wipe and smooth off excess joint compound with a 5- or 6-in. putty knife. Press the edge of the tape with the knife blade to ensure a tight bond with the drywall.**

8 Scrape away excess mud before it hardens. Scraping dried joint compound from the corner can damage the paper tape. Remove excess joint compound before it hardens. Carefully slide a putty knife along the outside edge to knock off excess joint compound.

ALIGN CORNERS

DRY JOINT COMPOUND

DAMAGED PAPER

6 Use staples to align corners. **Beads that intersect at corners have to align perfectly where they meet.** But without nails to hold them in place, the beads can slide out of position. The solution is to slide the corner bead into alignment with the adjoining bead and hold it in place with a few staples.

9 Finish up with two more coats of joint compound. After the embedding coat of mud is dry, apply another coat of joint compound and smooth it. Do a final coat after the second coat dries. Sand the corner with 150-grit drywall sandpaper mounted on a drywall sander. Sand carefully and only enough to blend the joint compound into the drywall and remove high spots. If you sand too much, you'll damage the paper face on the corner bead. If you do sand through the joint compound and create a fuzzy area, cover it with a thin layer of joint compound and resand when it dries.

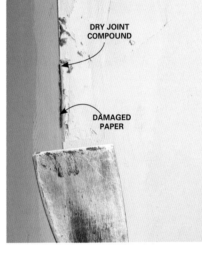

SECOND COAT

GreatGoofs®

No way out

I was relocating the shower in a bathroom that was built over a crawl space. To gain access, I cut a hole in the subfloor and slithered down between the joists with all my materials and tools. The floor would be an easy patch since I was retiling anyway. After I spent a few hours down there soldering copper pipes and gluing ABS drain lines, the new plumbing setup was perfect. Then it dawned on me that my beautiful new plumbing job blocked my way out through the opening. Unless I took the whole thing apart, I was trapped! I didn't have the heart to rip it all out, so I used my cell phone to call my son. I cooled my heels down there for an hour until he showed up and cut another hole in the floor to let me out.

Short-circuit shortcut

Mike, a carpenter buddy of mine, shared one of his cool remodeling tricks with me. When he comes across a hump in a wall caused by a badly bowed stud, he cuts right through the drywall and the stud with a long reciprocating saw blade. The cut relieves the stress and the stud straightens itself. Just a little patching to fix the saw kerf and you're done. Brilliant! I

had that exact problem in my downstairs bedroom—that hump had always driven me nuts.

I stuck the saw blade into the drywall and started hacking away. All of a sudden, the room went black and the saw stopped. The bad stud happened to be the one with electrical cable stapled to the side to feed the overhead light. I had cut through the cable and blown the circuit breaker. Needless to say, there was a lot more electrical work, drywall patching and painting ahead of me. But at least the wall was flat—mission accomplished!

Mysterious meowing

I volunteered to install a handicap shower for my uncle, who was recovering from knee surgery. To start, I framed in a corner of his bathroom. While I was working, his four cats were constantly underfoot, so I carried them out of the room.

I finished the framing, installed the shower and even built a couple of shelves in the corner. Then I went home, ate and settled down to watch football. Right after kickoff, my uncle called. He'd heard a meowing in the bathroom but couldn't figure out where it was coming from. You guessed it—one of the cats had somehow snuck back into the room and crawled into the space between the studs and the new shower just before I finished hanging the new drywall. I had to cut a hole in the wall to get Midnight out.

I guess I'll find out whether there's any bad luck in store for me for walling off a black cat in a bathroom.

A snag in the shag

A few years ago, I was installing bypass closet doors in a customer's newly finished basement, complete with beautiful, expensive new carpet. Everything was going fine until it was time to screw the door guides to the concrete floor. I got out my hammer drill to drill the pilot holes for the concrete screws.

In a split second, the drill bit grabbed a carpet fiber and ripped a perfectly straight snag right down the middle of the $30 a yard woven carpet. I had to recruit my friend the carpet expert to fix the problem—he said it happens to carpenters all the time. I just wish I had cut a little slit in the carpeting before drilling. Then I wouldn't have lost money on that job.

Sunroof disaster

I finally got around to replacing the flashing on one of our dormers. My extension ladder was too short to let me work comfortably at the peak of the dormer, so I drove my pickup into the front yard and placed the ladder in the bed, propping the bottom against the tailgate. It worked perfectly, giving me the extra height I needed.

I climbed up the ladder and went to work. No sooner had I gotten down to business than the hammer slipped out of my hand, ricocheted off the ladder rungs and smashed through the sunroof of my truck. A one in a million shot. To look on the bright side, at least it didn't go through my windshield. But from now on, I'll use scaffolding to work on the high points of my house.

Fastest way to unload lumber

I was at the home center, buying yet another load of materials to finish my basement. I strapped the lumber and copper pipe to my truck rack, then hit the highway.

All was well and good until I was almost home and a small dog darted into the street right in front of me, forcing me to slam on my brakes. My truck stopped, but my load didn't. The lumber and piping went flying off the rack, landing on the street. Luckily, there wasn't a car in front of me or it would have had an unexpected delivery through its back window. The dog ran away unscathed, but I swear he was laughing at me.

Painting Kitchen Cabinets

A fresh face for your cabinets

All it takes is two coats of paint!

You don't need to spend thousands of dollars on new cabinets to give your kitchen a stunning new look. If your cabinets are in good shape, you can give them a fresh face with paint. Everything you need to give your drab cabinets a silky smooth painted finish costs less than $250—including the sprayer.

Professional painters typically spray-paint doors because it produces an ultra-smooth finish. In this article, we'll show you how to spray-paint your doors and drawers. There's just a short learning curve to use the sprayer effectively. You could also spray the cabinet frames, sides and trim, but masking off the cabinet openings (and the rest of the kitchen) takes a lot of time, so just use a brush for those areas.

Despite our enthusiasm, there are downsides to a painted finish. The paint isn't as tough as a factory finish, and even if you're careful, you can still end up with paint runs and have brush marks on your cabinet sides.

All the materials you need to paint your cabinets are available at home centers and paint stores. Plan to spend four or five days to complete the job—you'll have to let the paint dry overnight between coats, and you can only paint one side of the doors per day.

New-looking cabinets in 3 steps

1. PREP
2. PRIME
3. PAINT

Is painting right for you?

Not all cabinets are worth painting. They must be structurally sound—paint obviously isn't a cure for doors that are falling apart or don't close properly. If your cabinets are oak or some other species with coarse grain and you want a smooth finish, you'll have to fill the grain on the door panels, cabinet frames and cabinet sides with spackling compound. That nearly doubles the length of this project, because sanding the compound takes a long, long time (but if you don't mind a coarse finish, you can skip this step).

If you like the style of your cabinets and they're in good shape, and you're willing to invest the time to paint them, this project is for you.

Wash, rinse, tape, repeat

As with any successful painting project, preparation is the key—and the most time-consuming step. Start by removing the cabinet doors and drawers as well as all the hardware. Label the doors as you remove them so you'll know where to reinstall them. Writing a number in the hinge hole (for Euro hinges) or where the hinge attaches works great—it's the only part that's not painted.

Take the doors and drawers to the garage or another work area and spread them out on a work surface. It's surprising how much space doors and drawers eat up—even if you have a small kitchen. An extension ladder placed over sawhorses gives you a surface to set the doors on. Wash the front and the back of the doors and the drawer fronts to remove grease (**Photo 1**). Then stick tape in the hinge holes or where the hinges attach to keep out the paint.

Wash the grease off the cabinet frames in the kitchen, too. Then tape off everything that abuts the cabinet frames (**Photo 2**). Use plastic sheeting ($13 for six 9 x 12-ft. sheets of 1-mil plastic) or brown masking paper ($3 for 12 in. x 60 yds.) to cover appliances. Use rosin paper ($12 for 3 ft. x 167 ft.) for countertops—it's thick enough to resist tears and won't let small paint spills seep through.

Give cabinets a fresh start with primer

Some cabinets, like ours, have a catalyzed lacquer finish that's very hard. Primer won't form a good bond to this surface unless you scuff it up first. First sand any damaged areas on the doors or cabinet frames with 320-grit sandpaper to remove burrs or ridges, then fill the areas with spackling compound (**Photo 3**).

Lightly sand the doors and cabinet frames, trim and sides with 320-grit sandpaper. Sand just enough to take off the shine—you don't need to sand off the finish. Vacuum the dust off the wood using a bristle attachment. Right before you're ready to apply the primer, wipe down the doors and frames with a tack cloth ($2 for a two-pack). Running the

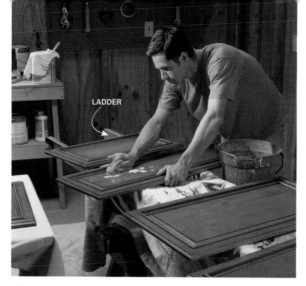

1 Wash off years of kitchen grease with warm water and dish detergent. Clean away all the grease or the primer and paint won't adhere. Rinse clean with water.

2 Tape off the walls, ceiling and flooring, and cover the countertops with rosin paper. Wrap appliances and the vent hood with plastic sheeting or masking paper.

cloth over the surface is enough—you don't need to scrub to remove the fine dust particles.

Apply a stain-killing primer ($20 per gal.; Bulls Eye 1-2-3 and BIN are two brands) with a paintbrush (**Photo 4**). You can use a cheap brush—even a disposable one—for this. Don't worry about brushstrokes in the primer (you'll remove them later with sandpaper) or getting a uniform finish. The doors and frames don't have to look pretty at this stage. But don't use a roller. It leaves a texture that will affect the finish. Besides, brushing is almost as fast as rolling, and you can use the bristles to work the primer into crevices.

Once the primer is dry (just one or two hours), lightly sand the doors and cabinets with 320-grit sandpaper to remove any brushstrokes (**Photo 5**). Sandpaper works better than a sanding sponge—you can feel the rough spots through the paper, and paper doesn't round over corners like sponges do.

SPACKLING COMPOUND

3 Fix scratches, holes and dings with spackling compound. Work the compound into the damaged area with a putty knife. Fill in holes from handles and hardware if you're replacing the hardware and need holes in different places.

4 Prime the doors and cabinet frames with stain-blocking primer. The primer covers any stains and seals in cooking odors. Prime one side of all the doors, let them dry while you prime the cabinet face frames and sides, then come back and prime the other side of the doors.

5 Sand the doors and cabinets with fine-grit sandpaper. Sand with the grain. Be careful not to round over corners. Wipe the surface clean with a tack cloth.

6 Start in a corner to paint the cabinet frames. Use a high-quality paintbrush to paint an entire rail or stile, including the inside edge, before moving to an adjacent rail or stile.

Immaculate finish in 90 minutes

For this project, we used a Wagner Control Spray Double Duty spray gun model No. 0518050; $90 at home centers. The high-volume, low-pressure (HVLP) sprayer gives the doors a thin, even coat of paint and makes quick work of painting. We sprayed our 18 doors and four drawers in less than 90 minutes per coat. The sprayer occasionally "spits" paint, but the Floetrol that you mix in levels out the finish. You can clean the sprayer in about 10 minutes.

The paint experts we talked to say you can get a nice-looking finish with non-HVLP sprayers too. But the advantages of an HVLP sprayer are that the low pressure produces little overspray, so most of your paint ends up where you want it—on the doors—and the spray is easy to control.

Figure A
Painting doors

Spray the door edges first. Then spray any detail work. Then spray the entire door, starting at the top and sweeping your arm back and forth until you reach the bottom. Keep the angle of the spray gun consistent as you spray.

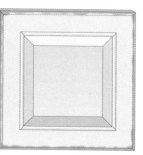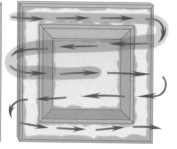

If you have doors with coarse wood grain (like oak) and want a smooth finish, fill in the grain with spackling compound (MH Ready Patch is one brand; $6 at home centers). Use a putty knife to skim-coat the door with compound, working it into the wood grain. Wait for it to dry, sand it with medium-grit sandpaper, then prime it again.

Complete the transformation with paint

Use a gloss or semigloss latex enamel paint for your cabinets. Its hard, shiny finish resists stains and fingerprints.

To get started, pour a gallon of the paint into a bucket and thin it with half a cup of water and half a quart of Floetrol paint additive ($9 per qt.). The water and the Floetrol level out the paint when it's applied and slow the drying process, which helps eliminate brush and lap marks. The thinner paint also provides a more even coat when you're spraying.

Paint the cabinets with a brush (**Photo 6**). Paint an entire rail, stile or trim piece before the paint dries, then move on to the next part of the cabinet. Paint any exposed sides of cabinets with a brush. Most light brush marks will disappear as the paint dries (thanks to the Floetrol).

Before spray painting, construct a makeshift booth to contain the airborne spray. Assemble a work surface (putting boards over sawhorses works great), then hang plastic sheeting around the work area. Make sure to ventilate the room—even if it's just a fan blowing out an open window.

Fill the spray container with the paint mixed with Floetrol and water. Wear a mask respirator ($8) when spray painting. Test the spray pattern on cardboard, keeping the nozzle 10 to 12 in. from the surface (**Photo 7**). Sweep your entire arm back and forth across the door panel; don't just use your wrist. Practice spraying on the cardboard to get a feel for the sprayer. When you're ready to paint, set a block of wood or a cardboard box on the work surface to elevate the doors. Place a lazy Susan turntable ($8 at discount stores) over the box, then set the door on top of it (**Photo 8**).

Spray the back of the doors first. This lets you get used to spraying before you paint the front. Start by spraying the edges. Rotate the door on the turntable to paint each edge so you won't have to change your body position. Move your

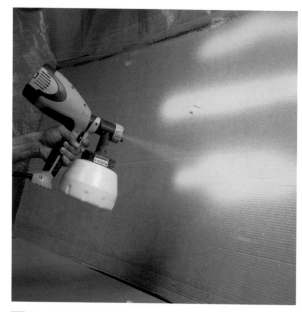

7 Practice spray painting on cardboard. Adjust the nozzle to get a vertical fan pattern. Adjust the flow rate so the paint covers the surface without running.

TURNTABLE

CARDBOARD BOX

8 Set the doors on a turntable when spray painting. Then you can stand in one spot and rotate the door to paint each side. Keep the nozzle 10 to 12 in. from the door and maintain a consistent angle while spraying.

9 Paint the edge and detail work on one side, then turn the door to paint the adjacent edges and details. Start the spray before the door, and keep spraying past the edge. Don't worry if you missed a spot. You can catch it on the second coat.

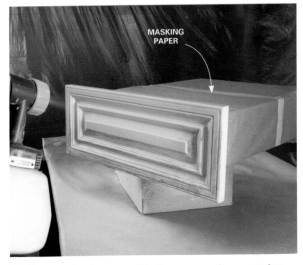

10 Paint the drawers with the sprayer after wrapping the inside with plastic or paper. Paint the backs first, then the edges and then the faces, starting at the top and working down. Start and stop the spray past the sides of the drawer.

11 Fix paint runs with a paintbrush while the paint is still wet. If the paint is dry or tacky, wait until the next day, then sand out the run or imperfection and repaint.

12 Reinstall the doors and drawers in the kitchen. Attach the hinges to the doors first, then screw them to the cabinet frames.

arm across the entire edge of the door, starting the spray before the paint lands on the door, and keep spraying past the end. Keep the nozzle 10 to 12 in. from the door. After painting all four edges, start at the top of the door and spray in a sweeping motion back and forth, moving down just enough each time to overlap the previous pass by 50 percent until you reach the door bottom.

Let the paint dry overnight. Then give the cabinet frames, sides and trim a second coat. Spray a first coat on the door fronts (**Photo 9**).

Cover the drawers with masking paper or plastic sheeting so only the paintable surface is visible. Set the drawer face down on the turntable and spray the back. Then place

the drawer on its bottom and spray the front (**Photo 10**). Be careful not to overspray the drawer. It's easy to get runs in the paint on drawer fronts. Don't worry about areas that are lightly covered. You'll give everything a second coat.

If you catch paint runs while they're still wet, gently brush them out with a paintbrush (**Photo 11**).

Let the doors and drawers dry overnight, then give them a second coat. It's up to you if you want to give the back of the doors two coats. We gave ours just one.

When the doors are dry, install the hardware and hang the doors (**Photo 12**). If any paint seeped into the hinge holes, scrape it out so the hinges will fit snugly.

2 Electrical & High-Tech

IN THIS CHAPTER

Question&Answer

SAVE A CUT EXTENSION CORD

I accidentally cut my good 100-ft. extension cord. A replacement costs almost $50! What's the best way to splice it back together so it's safe and doesn't pull apart?

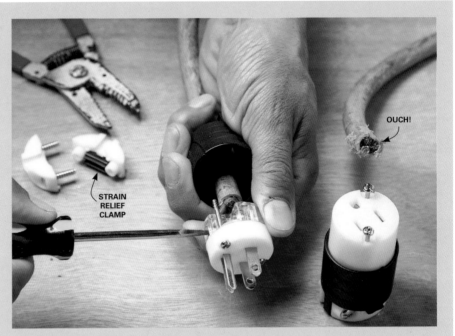

STRAIN RELIEF CLAMP

OUCH!

Technically, you're not supposed to splice extension cords. Even if you solder the wires, wrap each wire with electrical tape and encase the whole splice in heat shrinkable tubing, it still won't have the abrasion resistance of a new cord. Plus it's not permissible under the National Electrical Code.

If both sections are long enough to be worth saving, just buy a high-quality plug and receptacle and make two cords out of one. Be sure the new ends are rated to carry the same load as the old cord and that both have built-in strain relief clamps. Otherwise, just buy one end and accept the fact that your 100-ft. cord is now only 92.56 ft.

USING CFL BULBS IN GARAGE DOOR OPENERS

The lightbulb in my garage door opener burns out frequently. I want to install a CFL bulb for longer life and energy savings. But my neighbor claims that his opener "burned up" after he installed a CFL bulb. If I can't install a CFL, what do you recommend for longer bulb life?

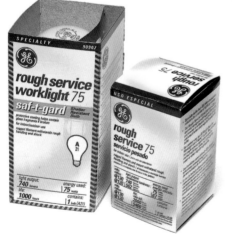

Pick up a standard rough-service bulb ($2.50) or a coated version ($5) at any home center.

We contacted the two largest residential garage door opener companies to ask about CFLs and possible damage to the opener. Both companies state that CFLs will not damage your opener. However, since electrical interference from the CFL ballast can reduce the operating range of your transmitter, they recommend always using an incandescent bulb.

Garage door openers produce a lot of vibration, so that's probably what's killing your bulbs. First tighten all the bolts on your unit and make sure it's solidly mounted to the ceiling. Then install a "rough service" bulb. These bulbs have heavy-duty filaments with extra support wires to keep them from breaking. Before anyone sends us letters about how "ungreen" incandescent bulbs are, wait a minute. The average opener light is on only a few minutes a day.

If your opener doesn't have a plastic lens, the bulb is unprotected, so choose a rough-service bulb with protective coating. The coating prevents the glass from shattering if it's ever struck.

HandyHints®

SLICK CHARGER I.D. TAGS

My electrical drawer was filled with chargers and transformers from our cameras, phones, portable vacuums and who knows what else. They all looked alike, and I could never find the one I needed in the tangled mess. Now I label each one we get, and I can find what I need instantly.

HOW MANY PIECES OF DUCT TAPE...

...does it take to change a lightbulb? One, if you fold it right. If you've ever tried to unscrew a lightbulb from a recessed fixture, you know how tough it is to get your fingers around it. Use duct tape to make a "handle." Rip a piece of duct tape off the roll and fold the ends back over themselves, leaving a sticky section in the middle. Put the sticky section on the bulb, grasp the ends and give the tape a twist. This trick works great—and that's no joke!

"HANDLE"

STICKY SECTION

ADD A CIRCUIT

...and live to tell about it

We believe in safe DIY. That's why we've always been reluctant to show readers how to open a breaker box and connect a new circuit. Even with the power shut off, there's a chance you could touch the wrong parts and kill yourself.

But then we figured if we didn't show you, you'd just go search the Internet. And that scared us even more. So we're going to walk you through the process, showing you the safest way to open the breaker box, wire a new breaker and test your work.

An inside look at your main panel

Opening the main breaker box and installing a new circuit is actually pretty easy. You only have to connect three wires, and each is color-coded. But there are some safety precautions, and if you ignore them, you could kill yourself. Really. If you follow our safety steps in order and to the letter, you'll be fine. But if at any point you're unsure how to proceed or feel uncomfortable with the project, call an electrician.

Stay away from the large wires and lugs. They're always live, even with the main breaker (service disconnect) shut off. If you touch them, you could die. Cover the live areas with a cardboard shield (**Photo 3**) to prevent accidental contact while installing the new circuit. If you have any doubts about which areas stay live, contact an electrician.

Your main panel might not be exactly like the one at right. The one shown above, for example, has the large cables and lugs at the right, rather than in the center. With any panel, find the large cables and the lugs they are connected to. They are the parts that are always live, even when the main breakers are switched off.

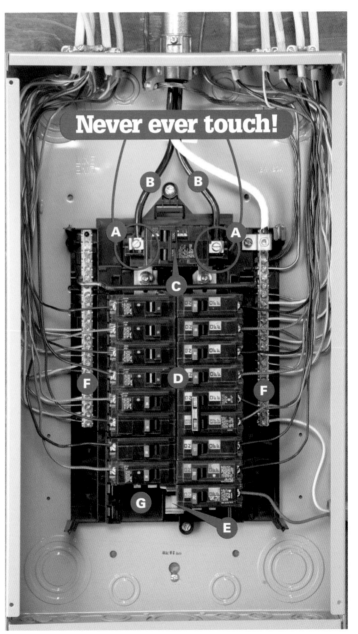

Get the right parts and tools

Before you go shopping, open the door of your breaker box and copy the manufacturer's name, the box model number, and the style numbers of the breakers that are approved for your box. Then buy one of those breakers. If your home center doesn't sell the right model or brand, you'll have to go to an electrical supplier. You cannot install a circuit breaker style that isn't specifically approved for use in your box—even if it fits inside the box. While at the store, pick up a few 1/2-in. plastic snap-in cable clamps to secure the new cable. They're safer than metal clamps, because you don't put your hand in the panel to install them.

You have to shut off the power to your whole house, so you'll need a powerful work light. An LED headlamp is also a great idea so you won't have to juggle a flashlight, wire strippers and a screwdriver. Round up a utility knife, wire strippers, electrical tape, a circuit tester (not a voltage sniffer), and a flat-blade screwdriver or No. 2 square-drive tip for your multi-bit driver.

Power down, then remove the cover

Turn off all computers in the house before you switch off the power. Then switch off the main breaker (the service disconnect) and follow the cover removal procedure in **Photo 1**.

Once the cover is off, cut out a cardboard shield and stick it inside the box to keep you from touching any of the live parts (see **Photo 3**).

It's dangerous to assume the power is really off just because you've flipped the service disconnect to the off position. There's a slim chance that the service disconnect didn't work properly, keeping power to some breakers. So test each and every breaker to make sure it's really dead (see **Photo 2**). If the test light lights up, stop and call an electrician.

Remove a knockout and feed in the cable

You can insert the new cable into any knockout on the top, bottom or sides of the box. Find the least congested area and remove one small knockout (**Photo 3**). Then snap in a plastic cable clamp (the screw-style ones shown aren't as easy to use).

1 **Don't break a breaker. Remove three of the panel cover screws. Then hold the cover securely while you remove the fourth screw. If it slips while you're removing screws, it can damage the breaker handles.**

NEUTRAL BUS

BREAKER SCREW

120V
240V
277V

2 **No light means no power. Be absolutely certain all the power is off. Touch one lead of a test light to the neutral bus and the other lead to the screw on each breaker.**

Know your way

Ⓐ **Main lugs.** They're always live—even when the main breaker is off. **NEVER TOUCH THEM.**

Ⓑ **Main cables.** The black ones are always live. And although they're insulated, avoid touching them.

Ⓒ **Main breaker.** Always switch it off before removing the panel's cover.

Ⓓ **Breaker.** The hot wire (usually red or black) from each circuit connects to a breaker. If you're installing an AFCI breaker (as shown on the following pages), you'll also connect the neutral wire to the breaker (Photo 7, p. 75).

Ⓔ **Breaker bus.** Distributes power from the main breaker to the individual circuit breakers. Each breaker snaps onto the bus (Photo 6, p. 74).

Ⓕ **Neutral bus.** All ground and neutral (white) wires connect here. If you're installing a standard breaker, the neutral (white) wire connects here, too. If you're installing an arc-fault circuit interrupter (AFCI) breaker, you'll connect the neutral to the breaker and run a "pigtail" wire to the neutral bus (Photo 8).

Ⓖ **Breaker space.** This panel has room for three more breakers. You can install your new breaker in any open space.

Hold the cable up to the box to determine how much of the outer jacket you should strip off. Slice off the jacket and remove the paper insulator. Then wrap the ends of the loose wires with electrical tape to prevent them from touching a live portion of the box (see **Photos 4 and 5**).

Route the cable and install the breaker

Neatly route the black and white wires to the empty breaker space. Attach the wires to the breaker and then snap it into the box, or install the breaker first and insert the wires last. Just be aware that wiring an AFCI-style breaker is different from wiring ordinary breakers. The neutral (white) from the new cable attaches to the AFCI (**Photo 7**). On a main panel, you connect the ground wire from the new cable and the neutral (white) pigtail from the AFCI to the neutral bus (**Photo 8**). If you're installing a breaker on a subpanel, place the neutral and ground on separate bus bars.

Test the installation and finish the job

Remove the panel cover plate knockout that corresponds to the slot where you installed the new breaker (bend it back and forth until it breaks off). Then install the cover and turn on the main breaker. Switch the new AFCI to "ON." Wait a few seconds and press the "TEST" button. The breaker should trip. If it doesn't trip, refer to the package instructions for troubleshooting or call an electrician.

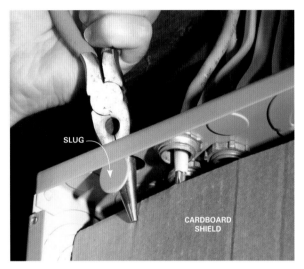

3 Smack it down, twist it out. **Jam needle-nose pliers or a short screwdriver into the knockout to bend it down. Then grab the "slug" with your pliers and twist it back and forth until it breaks off.**

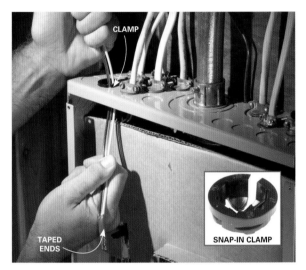

4 Run the cable through the clamp. **Snap in a plastic clamp and then feed in the cable. Tape the wires together so one doesn't stray behind the cardboard.**

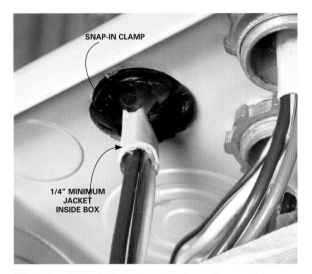

5 Push until the jacket enters the clamp. **Keep pushing the cable into the clamp far enough to get at least 1/4 in. of the outer jacket inside the box. Then secure the cable outside the box with an insulated staple within 12 in. of the clamp.**

6 Hook and push. **Install the breaker by slipping the tab into the hook. Then snap the breaker into place, forcing the slot onto the bus. We're using an AFCI breaker (see above).**

7 **Strip and clamp. Strip off 5/8 in. of insulation from the white and black wires and insert them into the AFCI** terminals. Tighten until snug.

8 Ground and pigtail go to the neutral bus. **Route the AFCI neutral pigtail and ground wires to empty screws on the neutral bus and tighten. If you're installing a breaker on a subpanel, place the neutral and ground on separate bus bars.**

How to plan a new branch circuit

DIYers often ask how many receptacles and lights they can install on a branch circuit and what size circuits they should install. We can give you some general guidelines, but electrical codes vary by state and local authority. Since your local codes always trump our advice, contact a local inspector before you start running cable.

1. You can usually mix lighting and receptacles on the same circuit. But it's not a good idea to place lighting and receptacles in the same room on a single circuit. If the breaker trips, you'll lose all the light fixtures and receptacles at the same time.
2. If you're wiring living areas, you can install 10 to 13 lights and receptacles on a single 15-amp circuit. Locate the receptacles so you're never more than 6 ft. away from one on each wall.
3. Run a separate 15- or 20-amp circuit for each of these watt-sucking appliances: garbage disposer, dishwasher, microwave, vent hood, trash compactor and space heater.
4. Run a separate 20-amp circuit to each bathroom and laundry room. Install a minimum of two 20-amp circuits for the kitchen. Protect the receptacles with a ground-fault circuit interrupter (GFCI) breaker or GFCI-style receptacles.
5. Use 12-gauge cable for 20-amp circuits and 14-gauge for 15-amp. Many cable manufacturers color-code the outer jacket of their cable, but the color schemes are not universal. So always double-check the wire itself to be sure (see photo at right).
6. New branch circuits to all "living areas" (bedroom, living room, family room, den, dining room, library, sunroom, closet, hallway and similar locations) must be connected to an arc-fault circuit interrupter (AFCI). AFCI breakers are pricey ($40), so you may be tempted to buy an ordinary $5 breaker. Don't. The electrical inspector will just make you change it out.

Check wire gauge with your loose change

Fourteen-gauge wire is the thickness of a dime; 12-gauge is the thickness of a nickel.

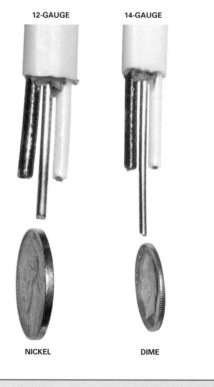

12-GAUGE   14-GAUGE

NICKEL   DIME

LIGHT UP A DARK ROOM

Is your bathroom dimly lit? Do you have a hallway that could use more light? Here's how to add a wall-mounted light directly above a light switch.

This project requires an understanding of how a switch is wired and a few basic tools. You'll need a noncontact voltage detector ($10), a wire-stripping tool ($6 to $15), a screwdriver and a drywall saw. Then, with our instructions and a few hours' work, you'll be able to add a sconce to any room that has an appropriate switch.

Not all electrical boxes with a light switch in them contain the necessary ground, hot and neutral conductors. To find out, first shut

off the power to the switch at the main electrical panel. Then remove the switch cover, and hold the non-contact voltage detector against the wires attached to the switch. This is to ensure the power is off before you remove the screws and pull the switch from the box.

You can add a sconce above nearly any light switch in about three hours.

To locate the required neutral, look for two or more white wires joined with a wire connector. If the only white wire entering the box is connected to the switch, then there's no neutral and you can't power a sconce from this box. If your switch wiring looks different from what we show here and you don't understand how it's connected, put everything back together and abandon the project or call a licensed electrician.

There's one more important test you must complete while the power is still turned on. With the light switch turned off, hold the noncontact voltage detector against each of the wires connected to the switch. Take note of which wire causes the tester to light up. This is the hot wire and the one you'll connect to the "hot" side of the new double switch. If you're adding a separate single switch, this is the wire you'll use to power both switches. Now turn off the power to the switch at the main electrical panel. Back at

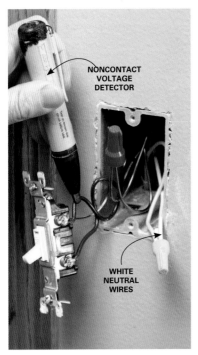

NONCONTACT VOLTAGE DETECTOR

WHITE NEUTRAL WIRES

1 Test for power. With the power turned off at the main electrical panel, unscrew the switch and pull it out. Turn the power back on and use a noncontact voltage tester to locate the hot wire.

CUTOUT FOR REMODELING BOX

2 Cut the hole. Trace around the box. Then draw a second line inside the first to indicate the cutout. Cut notches for clamps and other protrusions.

the switch box, *test once again to make sure the power is off* and mark the hot wire with a wrap of black electrical tape.

Finally, complete a simple calculation to see if the existing switch box is large enough to accept more wires. For instructions, go to familyhandyman.com and type "electrical wiring" into the search box.

After you've determined that the existing switch box will work to power the new light, it's time to shop for the sconce and pick up the remodeling box, cable and electrical connectors you'll need. Choose the fixture first. Then pick a rectangular or round remodeling box that is small enough to be covered by the light fixture canopy. You'll need enough cable to reach from the switch to the box plus about 3 ft. Match the cable, either 14-2 or 12-2, to the existing wire gauge. Fourteen-gauge wire is as thick as a dime and 12-gauge wire is as thick as a nickel (see p. 75).

Cut the hole and run the cable

Locate the studs. Then hold the fixture against the wall somewhere between the studs to determine the best location and lightly mark the top and bottom of the canopy with a pencil. Center the remodeling box on the marks and mark the box cutout carefully, taking note of notches needed for the clamps and other protrusions. Cut out the hole (**Photo 2**). Next punch out one of the knockouts in the top of the switch box and push the cable up to the hole (**Photos 3 and 4**). Prepare the remodeling box for mounting by stripping about 12 in. of sheathing from the cable and pushing it into the box through one of the cable entry points on the back. Make sure at least 1/4 in. of sheathing is visible inside the box. Leave some slack cable inside the wall to allow some leeway when you connect the switch (**Photo 5**). Then fit

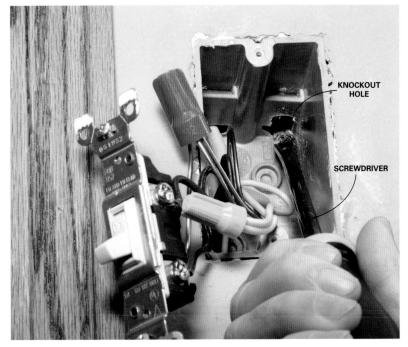

3 **Remove the knockout.** **Punch out one of the knockouts in the top of the box with a screwdriver. You'll push the cable through this hole.**

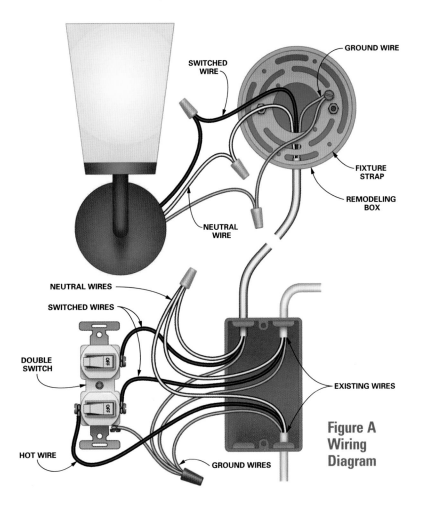

**Figure A
Wiring
Diagram**

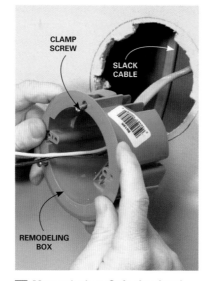

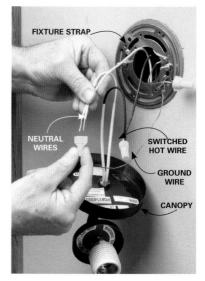

4 Push in the cable. Push the cable through the knockout and up toward the hole. If you're lucky, it'll come into sight. Otherwise, reach through the hole to grab it.

What if you have to go fish?

We're showing how to run a cable through the same stud space that contains the switch. Positioning the light in an adjacent stud space is more difficult. For information on how to do this, go to familyhandyman.com and type "fishing electrical wires" into the search box.

the remodeling box into the hole and tighten the clamps.

Connect the fixture and switch

Photo 6 and Figure A show how to connect the light fixture. Start by mounting the fixture strap to the box. Strip the ends of the wires and connect them to the fixture.

At the switch, cut the cable about 12 in. beyond the box. Strip 8 in. of sheathing from the wires and push the cable through the knockout, leaving 1/4 in. or more sheathing visible inside the box. Trim the black and white wires to the same length as the wires they will connect to. Then strip the ends of the wires. Connect the white neutral wires with a wire connector. Connect the wires as shown in **Figure A**. Connect the hot wire to the side of the double switch that has the "jumper tab" between the terminals (**Photo 7**). Complete the project by mounting the light fixture, screwing the switch to the box, and installing the cover plate.

5 Mount the box. Strip the sheathing from about 12 in. of cable. Push the wires through the built-in wire clamp at the back of the box. Make sure at least 1/4 in. of sheathing is visible inside the box. Push the box into the hole and tighten the clamp screws.

6 Install the fixture. Trim the black and white wires to 8 in., leaving the ground wire long. Strip the ends of the wires. Connect white to white, black to black and bare copper to bare copper. Loop the bare copper wire clockwise around the grounding screw on the fixture strap before connecting it to the fixture ground wire.

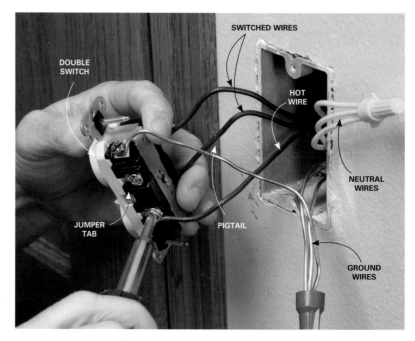

7 Connect the switch. Strip the ends of the wires at the switch box. Connect the neutral white wires with a wire connector. Connect the ground wires with a 6-in.-long pigtail wire leading to the switch. Loop the black wires clockwise around the screws and tighten the screws.

3 Plumbing, Heating & Appliances

IN THIS CHAPTER

REPAIR YOUR LEAKING WATER DISPENSER

If you have a water dispenser in the door of your refrigerator and notice water on the floor when you fill a glass, the vinyl tubing that runs under the refrigerator could be leaking. To find out, pull the refrigerator forward a little. Then tip it back and prop up the front feet on blocks of wood. Look underneath and ask someone to dispense a glass of water. If the tube's leaking, you'll see it.

The fix is simple. **Photos 1 – 3** show the steps. Cut out the section of damaged tubing and take it with you to the home center or hardware store. Buy a new section of vinyl tubing and one or two quick-connect couplings. If you don't have a quick-connect coupling on one end of the damaged tube as shown in **Photo 1**, then cut the tubing in two spots and join it with two new quick-connect couplings.

The tubing for icemakers can also get damaged and leak. So if you ever notice water on the floor under your refrigerator, check for a leaking tube and repair it using the process we show here.

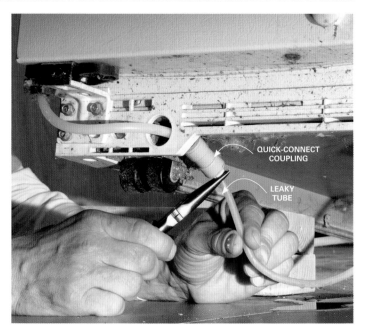

1 **Disconnect the leaking tube. Disconnect one end of the leaking tube by pressing in on the inner ring with needle-nose pliers to release the tube. If there isn't a quick-connect coupling, simply cut the tube with a sharp utility knife.**

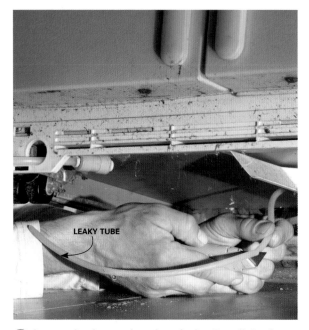

2 **Cut out the damaged section of tube. Cut off the damaged tubing with a sharp utility knife. Don't use a side cutters; it'll distort the tubing and prevent a good seal with the quick-connect coupling.**

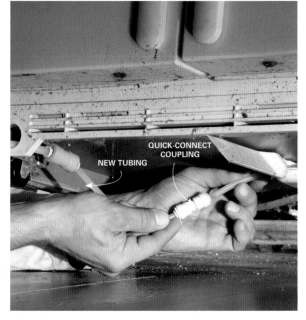

3 **Splice in a new section of tubing. Quick-connect couplings simplify this repair. Just push cut ends of the tubing into the coupling for a leak-free connection.**

SLOW-FLOWING SPRAYER

If your pullout sprayer delivers a weak spray, here's what to do. First, make sure the problem is with the spray head and not farther down the line. Start by removing the sprayer (Photo 1). Clip a clothespin or small clamp on the hose to keep it from snaking back down the spout. If water flows from the hose when you turn on the faucet, then you know the problem is in the spray head—unless the flow is still weak. In that case, there's a problem with the faucet or supply lines. Go to familyhandyman.com and type "faucet repair" into the search box for help with this problem.

Most pullout sprayers have an inlet screen (Photo 2), a removable aerator (Photo 4) or both, which can get clogged with mineral deposits or other debris. But there are dozens of different types of pullout spray faucets, and they all have slightly different parts, so yours may not look exactly like this. The biggest difference is in how you remove the aerator. On some faucets, the aerator has flat spots for a wrench or pliers and you simply unscrew it (Photo 4). Other faucets require a special tool (sometimes included with new faucets) for unscrewing the aerator. You can clean out the holes in the inlet screen with a dental pick or other pointed tool (Photo 2), but it's not worth trying to clean a clogged aerator since they seldom work quite right when you're done. Take the aerator to a hardware store, home center or plumbing supplier to find a replacement. If it's not available, go to the manufacturer's Web site to find out how to order one.

If these fixes don't work or you don't want to do them, simply replace the entire spray head. First contact the manufacturer of your faucet. It may be guaranteed so that you can get a new spray head free. If not, go to the manufacturer's Web site for information on ordering a new one (it will cost about $30 to $40). Also many home centers stock a generic replacement that fits most faucets (about $25).

PLUMBING, HEATING & APPLIANCES

HOSE

1 Unscrew the sprayer. **Turn off the water at the faucet and use pliers to loosen the nut that holds the sprayer to the flexible hose. Remove the sprayer. Hold the tube facing down into the sink and gradually turn on the water at the faucet to check the water pressure.**

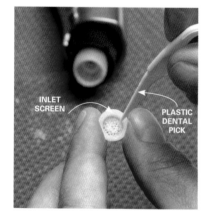

INLET SCREEN

PLASTIC DENTAL PICK

2 Clean the inlet screen. **Look down into the hose end of the sprayer and see if there's a small screen. If there is, remove it by tapping the sprayer or gently prying it out with a small pointed tool. Clean the holes with a toothpick or plastic dental pick.**

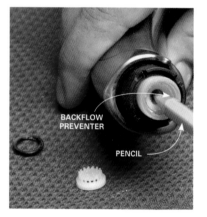

BACKFLOW PREVENTER

PENCIL

3 Check the backflow preventer. Inspect the area under the inlet screen to see if there's a backflow preventer. Gently press a pencil against this round disc to make sure it moves freely. Clean off any mineral deposits around the edges.

AERATOR

4 Check the aerator. **Unscrew the aerator with pliers or a wrench.** Some pullout spray heads don't have removable aerators. Ask the manufacturer if you can't tell.

HomeCare & Repair

WASHING MACHINE WON'T DRAIN?

If the water won't drain out of your washing machine, either something is stuck in the drain hose or pump, or the pump is broken. Both fixes are simple if you're even just a little bit handy with tools. We're showing the repair on a Maytag washing machine.

Start by unplugging the machine and emptying the water. Bail the water out of the tub, or you can drain the tub using gravity by placing the drain hose on the floor near the drain or in a bucket. Clamp the hose to prevent any remaining water from running out (**Photo 3**). Once the washer's empty, support the front of it on paint cans or stacked 2x4s. **Photo 1** shows where to find the screws that hold the front panel in place. Remove the panel and you'll see the pump. The pump has a translucent housing, so you might even see the offending piece of clothing wrapped up in the pump. **Photo 3** shows what to do if the pump is clogged. If you don't see the clog in the pump or in the hose near the pump, then it could be stuck in the outlet where the hose connects to the bottom of the tub.

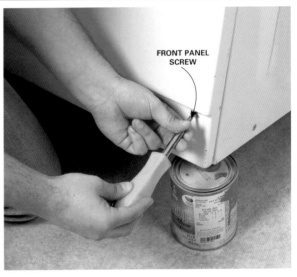

1 Remove panel screws. **Unplug the washer. Then prop up the washer and remove the two screws that secure the front panel.**

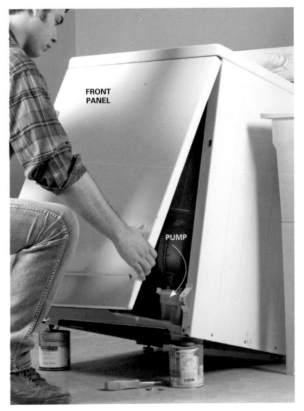

2 Remove the front panel. **Pull the lower edge of the panel outward and "unhook" the top. On a Whirlpool washer, you'll have to remove the entire shell to access the pump.**

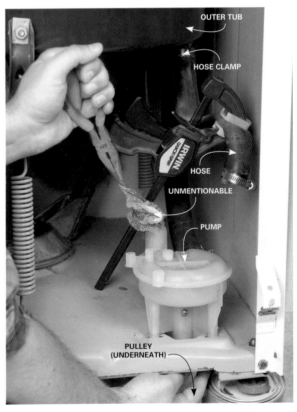

3 Pull out the clog. **Remove the belt from the pulley on the bottom side of the pump. It's spring-loaded, so it comes off easily. Then remove the hose, and if the clog is visible, pull it out. Twist the pulley to unwind the fabric as you pull it out.**

To find out, loosen the clamp that holds the hose to the bottom of the tub and remove the hose. Have a bucket and sponge handy, though. Any water that's left in the machine will run out. When you locate the piece of clothing, pull it out with needle-nose pliers.

If nothing is clogging the hose or pump, the pump could be shot, although in most cases you'll hear noise from a bad pump, and it'll start to leak if you don't replace it right away. **Photo 4** shows how to remove the pump. Buy a new one to match. You can find a new pump online or go to your local appliance parts center. You'll need the brand and model number for proper part identification. Model numbers are usually stamped on a small metal plate located under the tub lid or on the top, side or back of the machine. Copy down all the plate information and use it to access online parts suppliers, or take it along to the parts distributor. Install the new pump by attaching it with screws and connecting the hoses, and then reinstall the belt.

4 Remove the pump. **If the impeller inside the pump is damaged (reach your finger inside to feel for broken fins) or if the pump leaks or makes noise, you'll have to replace it. Remove the three screws that hold the pump to the washer. Buy a new pump and install it.**

FIX YOUR DRIPPING LAUNDRY FAUCET

Laundry faucets like this are easy and cheap to fix. If it's dripping from the spout, you need a new faucet washer. And if water is leaking around the handle, the rubber O-ring around the valve stem is bad. But since you have to take out the valve stem for either repair, and the fix is simple, we recommend replacing both the hot and cold washers and the O-rings while the faucet is apart. Remember to turn off the water and purge the pressure before you start. If you're lucky, there'll be a separate shutoff for the laundry room. Otherwise, you'll have to shut off the water to the whole house by closing the main valve.

Photos 1 and 2 show how to do the repair. After you've removed the valve stems, take them to the hardware store. You'll find drawers full of faucet washers and O-rings. Just find washers that will fit snugly in the recess, and matching O-rings. If you damaged the screw that holds the washer on when you removed it, buy new brass screws. Now simply reassemble everything in the reverse order. No more drips!

1 Unscrew the valve. **Remove the handle. Then turn the valve counterclockwise with a wrench. Pull out the valve.**

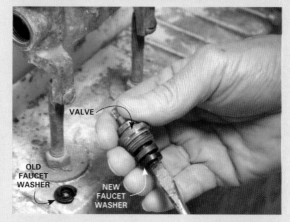

2 Replace the washer. **Remove the screw that holds the washer to the valve. Install the new washer and replace the screw.**

UNCLOG A BATHROOM SINK— WITHOUT CHEMICALS

Slow-moving or stopped-up drains are common in bathroom sinks, but luckily the fix is usually simple and takes only about 15 minutes. The problem is caused by hair and gummy soap scum that get caught on the stopper or pivot rod and clogs the drain.

To get at the clog, try lifting out the stopper (**Photo 1**). Sometimes it'll come right out. If it doesn't lift out, it's held in by the pivot rod. Release the stopper by removing the pivot rod nut and pulling out the pivot rod (**Photo 3**). If you can't loosen the nut by hand, use pliers. With the pivot rod pulled out, you'll be able to lift out the stopper. Then to get the clog out, bend a wire in a tight hook (a light-duty clothes hanger or short length of electrical wire will do) and fish out the hair (**Photo 2**). If you didn't have to remove the pivot rod to remove the stopper, you can just drop the stopper back down into the drain. If you removed the pivot rod, first drop the stopper into the drain. Then line up the pivot rod with the slot in the stopper and reinsert it. Finally, hand-tighten the pivot rod nut.

Run hot water down the drain to help clear out any remaining soap scum and to check that the clog is gone. Check around the pivot rod nut to make sure it's not leaking. If you see drips, tighten the pivot rod nut slightly with pliers.

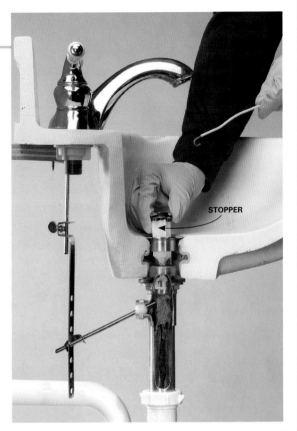

1 If the stopper comes out: **Tug on the stopper to see if it'll come out. If so, remove it.**

STOPPER

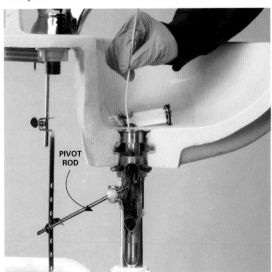

2 Remove the clog. **Fish out the hair clog with a bent wire or other tool. Run water through the drain and replace the stopper.**

PIVOT ROD

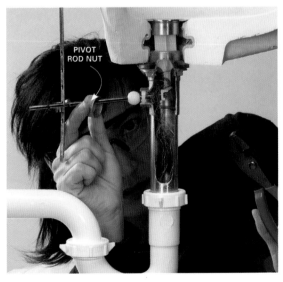

3 If the stopper doesn't come out: **Unscrew the pivot rod nut and pull out the rod. Lift out the stopper. Clean out the hair and reinstall the stopper and pivot rod.**

PIVOT ROD NUT

DRY CLOTHES QUICKER WITH A DRYER DUCT BOOSTER

If it takes forever for your clothes to dry, the problem could be the dryer duct. A dryer vent duct that's too long reduces the airflow and wastes energy. Most dryer manufacturers recommend a maximum duct length of about 25 ft. But the catch is that every bend in the pipe is equivalent to about 5 ft. of straight pipe. It adds up quickly.

A company called Tjernlund Products (search online for "Tjernlund duct booster") has a solution. For about $250, you can buy a dryer duct booster that switches on automatically when it senses airflow through the duct. The booster also has a specially designed fan that won't clog with lint, unlike less expensive boosters.

Mount the booster to the wall or ceiling at least 10

ft. from the dryer and in the path of the existing vent. Connect the vent to the booster and plug it in.

FIX FOR A RUNNING TOILET

If you hear your toilet refilling too often, or if you hear the steady hiss of running water, the flapper may be leaking. The flapper (aka "flush valve seal") is the plug that falls against the drain hole (flush valve drain seat) on the bottom of the tank and holds water in until the next time you flush. When flappers or flush valve seats wear out, water trickles out, causing the water valve to open to refill the tank. Usually the fix is simple. Remove the old flapper and take it with you to the hardware store or home center to find a matching replacement.

Occasionally a new flapper doesn't solve the problem. If you've tried replacing the flapper but the toilet still runs, the flush valve seat is probably rough or pitted. You can replace the entire flush valve, but it's a big job. Here's an easier fix. Look for a flapper kit that contains a flush seat repair. We show a Fluidmaster 555C kit ($7), but others are available. The kit contains a flapper and matching seat that you adhere to the damaged seat with the adhesive provided, as shown.

Start by closing the valve on the

water line to the toilet by turning it clockwise. Then flush the toilet and hold the flapper open to allow the water to drain from the tank. Use a sponge to mop out the water that remains. Follow the included instructions to install the new valve seat and flapper. The Fluidmaster flapper we show includes a plastic cup that allows you to adjust the length of time the flapper stays open. It's for toilets that use 3.5 gallons or less for a flush. If your toilet uses more than this, remove the timing cup. Install the new flapper. Then adjust the length of the chain so it's just slightly slack when the flapper is down. Turn on the water and test the flush. You may have to fiddle with the length of the chain to get the flapper working correctly. When you're done, cut off the excess chain to keep it from getting stuck under the flapper.

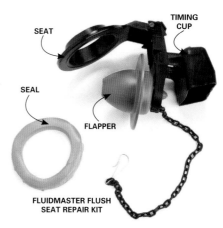

FLUIDMASTER FLUSH SEAT REPAIR KIT

Repair the flush seat. Follow the directions included with your flush seat repair kit to seal a new repair seat onto the old, damaged seat.

UNCLOG A KITCHEN SINK

BENT COAT
HANGER

WASTE
TEE

BAFFLE

POTATO
PEELS

When the water in your kitchen sink won't drain or drains slowly, don't reach for the chemical drain cleaner. Instead, try this three-step method recommended by one of our favorite plumbers. The first two steps we'll show you don't even require you to remove the trap or take anything apart. If you're lucky, all you'll need is a bent coat hanger. But if the clog is in the trap or farther down the drain, you'll need a 1/4-in. drain snake. You can buy an inexpensive snake that's

simply a cable running through a bent pipe that allows you to twist the cable, but we recommend spending a little more money for a cable that's enclosed in a drum ($15 to $40). This type is much easier to use.

Before you get started on any of our solutions, suck all the water out of the sink with a wet-dry shop vacuum or sponge it into a bucket. You'll be able to see what you're doing, and if you do have to disassemble plumbing, it'll be less messy.

Never have another clog!

Garbage disposers and grease are the two biggest contributors to clogged sink drains. Here's the first rule for avoiding clogs: Don't use your garbage disposer like a trash can. If your family sends vast amounts of food down the disposer, you'll have a clogged sink someday. Disposing of turkey carcasses, gummy foods like pasta and fibrous items like banana peels in the sink is asking for trouble. The same goes for heaping plates of leftovers. Scrape the big stuff into the garbage can and use the disposer for the small stuff.

The second rule: Never pour grease down the drain. And running hot water along with it won't help. The grease will just congeal farther down the drainpipe where it'll be even harder to clear.

STEP 1: The coat-hanger trick

If you have a two-bowl sink and only one side is clogged, there's a good chance this fix will work. First look under the sink to locate the waste tee. If your drain setup looks something like the one shown here and the water is backing up on the side without the waste tee, you may be able to remove the clog with a bent coat hanger (**opening photo**). There's a baffle inside the waste tee that is meant to direct water down the drain, but since the baffled area is narrower than the rest of the drain, food often gets stuck there. Garbage disposers are notorious for causing clogs, especially at the baffle.

The trick is to bend a hook on the end of a coat hanger wire and use it to dislodge the clog. Use pliers to bend a hook that will fit through the slots in the basket strainer. Peek under the sink to get a rough idea how far down the waste tee is from the basket strainer. Push the bent hanger down the drain. Then twist and pull until you feel it hook onto the baffle. Now wiggle it up and down while twisting it to remove the clog. Run water in the clogged sink to tell if you've removed the obstruction. If the sink still doesn't drain, there's a clog farther down. Move on to Step 2.

STEP 2: Run a snake through the basket strainer

There are several advantages to this approach. You don't have to remove all the stuff from under the sink, struggle to take apart and reassemble drains, or worry about spilling dirty drain water when you remove the trap. Also pushing the cable down through the basket strainer allows you to clean the slime-covered cable as you withdraw it by running clean water down the drain. (Believe me, this is a nice bonus!) And finally, since the drain is still fully assembled, you'll be able to tell, by running water in the sink, whether you've unclogged the drain.

You have to modify the end of the cable on your drain snake to use this method, however (**photo below**). Then you snake out the drain by pushing the cable down through one of the slots or holes in the basket strainer. See "The Art of Running a Snake" on p. 88.

1/4" DRAIN SNAKE

BENT END

TRAP

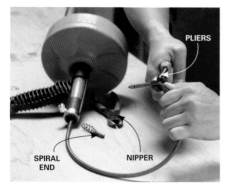

PLIERS

SPIRAL END

NIPPER

Modify your drain snake to fit through the slot in the basket strainer. First clip off the spiral end. Then bend the last few inches at about a 30-degree angle with pliers. Finally, unwind the tip slightly to form a small hook.

If the bent coat hanger doesn't get the clog, there's a good chance you can clear it without taking your plumbing apart. Run a modified snake (see photo, left) down through the slots in the basket strainer.

STEP 3: Take the trap apart

If you can't unclog the drain using Steps 1 or 2, then it's time to take off the trap and waste arm and feed the drain snake directly into the drainpipe. Remember to remove as much water from the sink as possible before you remove the trap. Then place a bucket under the trap to catch any remaining water. Use large slip-joint pliers to loosen the slip-joint nuts on both ends of the trap. Unscrew the nuts and remove the trap. Do the same with the nut that secures the waste arm to the drain and remove the waste arm.

Before you reach for the drain snake, look up into the baffle tee to make sure the baffle area is clear. Then look into the trap to make sure there's no clog in the bottom. If both spots are clear, then the clog is farther down in the drainpipe and you'll need a drain snake.

With this method, the only way you'll know if you've unclogged the drain is to reassemble the trap and run water down the drain. If you've got a metal trap and drain arm, we recommend replacing them and the other metal drain parts with plastic. Plastic parts are easy to cut and assemble. They're also easier to take apart if you have a problem in the future, and they don't corrode.

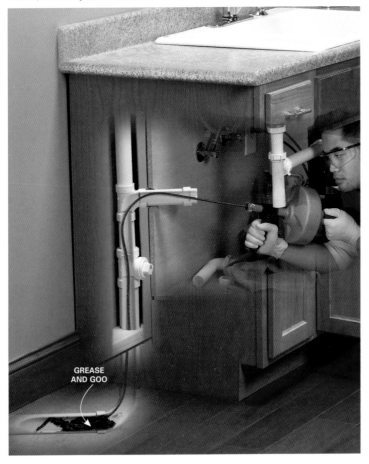

GREASE AND GOO

If the previous two approaches didn't work, remove the trap and waste arm to get to the clog. You'll have two fewer bends to get around with the snake and have an easier time reaching deep clogs.

The art of running a snake

There's an art to using a drain snake, and the more experience you have, the better you'll be at it. Here's how you do it. Loosen the setscrew or chuck to allow the cable to come out of the drum freely. Now feed the cable into the drain until you can't push it any more. It may be stuck on the clog or simply meeting resistance where the drainpipe bends.

Position the end of the drum so there's about 8 in. of cable showing between the drain and the drum, and tighten the setscrew or chuck onto the cable. Withdraw the cable about an inch so that it's free of the obstruction, and start turning the drum while you push it toward the drain. Continue until you've pushed the exposed cable down the drain. Then repeat the process by loosening the setscrew and withdrawing another 8 in. of cable. If the end of the cable gets stuck and you keep turning the drum, the cable will start to spiral inside the drain. You want to avoid this, so stop turning the drum if you feel that the cable isn't turning freely anymore. Withdraw the cable about 6 in. and try again.

Several things can happen at this point. You might bore through the clog, allowing water to run through and dissolve the remaining clog. You might push the clog to a point where the diameter of the pipes is larger and it can wash down the drain. Or you might hook the clog with the end of the snake and pull it out. This is where your intuition comes into play. When you think you've unclogged the drain, withdraw the snake. If you've pushed the cable down through the basket strainer, you can rinse it off as you retrieve it by running water. Otherwise, put on some gloves and wipe the cable off with a rag as you push it back into the drum.

When you're done cleaning the drain, pull the cable out of the drum, rinse it off, and wipe it down with an oil-soaked rag to keep it from rusting.

PEX
EDUCATION

Gary Wentz explains everything you always wanted to know but were afraid to ask

I'm not a plumber. But like any remodeler, I occasionally find myself relocating a hose bib or fixing a pipe that managed to get in the way of my Sawzall. For years, my plumbing kit was a torch and a bucket of copper fittings. These days, that bucket mostly holds PEX fittings and tools. And my soldering torch doesn't get used much anymore.

Switching to PEX wasn't difficult; PEX is a whole lot easier to master than copper. The only tricky part was deciding what to carry in my plumbing bucket. Visiting the plumbing aisle at my local home center didn't help matters—all those strange tools, connection systems and unfamiliar thingamajigs made my head spin. But with lots of advice and a little on-the-job training from plumber friends, I figured out what's needed and what isn't. Here's what I learned about getting set up for PEX.

PEX costs less than half the price of copper and installs much faster. And since it's flexible, PEX makes remodeling jobs easier.

LESSON 1: Choose a common connection system

Before you choose a system for connecting PEX to fittings, check what's available at the stores where you like to shop. There are a half-dozen systems out there, but most are available only through specialty plumbing suppliers. If you want to shop at home centers and hardware stores, there are two widely available methods to choose from: copper crimp rings and stainless steel cinch rings. I like the cinch system better, because the tool ($45) is smaller and one tool can handle four ring sizes (3/8 to 1 in.). But cinch rings aren't as widely available in my area, so I chose the crimp system instead. Crimp rings require a different tool for each size (and each tool costs at least $50) or a combination tool ($100), and the bigger tools are awkward in tight spots. Still, I'd rather put up with the drawbacks of the crimp system than drive across town to get supplies. If you want to shop online, pexsupply.com is a good place to start. Whatever system you choose, keep an eye on prices: I've found that the costs vary a lot from one supplier to another.

CINCH RINGS
Cinch rings tighten as you pinch the tab with the tool.

CRIMP RINGS
Crimp ring connections are made by compressing a copper ring around the PEX and fitting.

LESSON 2: Buy sticks, not coils

PEX has a strong "memory"; it always wants to spring back to its original shape. So working with a coil of PEX is like wrestling with a giant Slinky. For most jobs, you're better off buying 10-ft. "sticks" instead ($2.50 each for 1/2-in. diameter). You may have to pay a few cents more per foot and install a coupler or two, but you'll avoid frustration and kinks. Even plumbers who run miles of PEX every year often buy sticks rather than coils.

Coils are great when you have lots of long runs, but straight "sticks" are a lot easier to use. The red and blue colors eliminate hot-and-cold confusion.

LESSON 3: Stock up on push-ins

Don't begin any PEX job without a few push-in elbows, tees and couplings (SharkBite is one brand; sharkbite.com). They're the best solution for cramped quarters where there's no space for a crimping or cinching tool. No tool is needed; just push in the PEX and walk away. Push-in fittings also work with copper and CPVC. Convenience doesn't come cheap, though. You'll spend from $5 to $12 per fitting. Also check with your local inspector before you use push-in fittings. Some jurisdictions don't allow them in inaccessible locations like inside walls.

Push-in fittings work with copper and CPVC as well as with PEX.

LESSON 4: Bend PEX carefully—or not at all

PEX is easy to kink. With one brand (Uponor Wirsbo), you can restore the tubing by heating it. But with most PEX, you have to cut out the kink and splice in a new section. You can also damage PEX by overbending it. (The minimum bend radius is typically six to eight times the outer diameter, depending on the manufacturer.) One way to avoid kinking and overbending is to use bend sleeves ($2). Keep in mind that—even with a sleeve—a bend requires open working space. In tight situations, save yourself some struggling by using an elbow fitting instead.

A bend sleeve prevents kinking or creating a too-tight bend.

LESSON 5: Get a crimp cutter

PEX fittings cost about three times as much as copper fittings. So you won't want to toss your mistakes in the trash. If you use cinch rings, you can saw or twist off the ring tab, pull off the PEX and reuse the fitting. But sawing through a crimp ring—without damaging the fitting—is a job for a surgeon. For the rest of us, a crimp cutter ($25) is a lifesaver. Just slice off the PEX flush with the fitting and make two cuts in the ring.

A crimp cutter lets you remove crimp rings without damaging the fitting.

LESSON 6: Stub out with copper

You can buy shutoff valves that connect directly to PEX. But don't. PEX can't handle abuse the way copper can—for example, from cramming more and more stuff into a vanity or cranking that crusty valve closed years from now. So use copper rather than PEX for wall stub-outs. For risers coming out of the floor (or extending down from the ceiling to a laundry tub faucet), use lengths of copper pipe.

Copper stub-outs ($5) provide a PEX connection on one end and solid support for shutoff valves on the other.

GreatGoofs®

Two times the water damage

The toilet in the upstairs bathroom had been leaking for some time, which had rotted the floor. I removed the toilet, vanity and sink to replace the plywood. Once the new vinyl floor and the vanity were installed, I left off the sink to make it easier to solder on new shutoff valves.

With the main water supply to the house turned off, I installed the shutoff valves. Then I went downstairs to turn on the water supply so I could check the joints for leaks. As I walked back upstairs, fancying myself a master plumber, I heard the sound of gushing water. I had forgotten to turn off the shutoff valves! The bathroom was flooded and the ceiling below was ruined. But my soldering job held up perfectly.

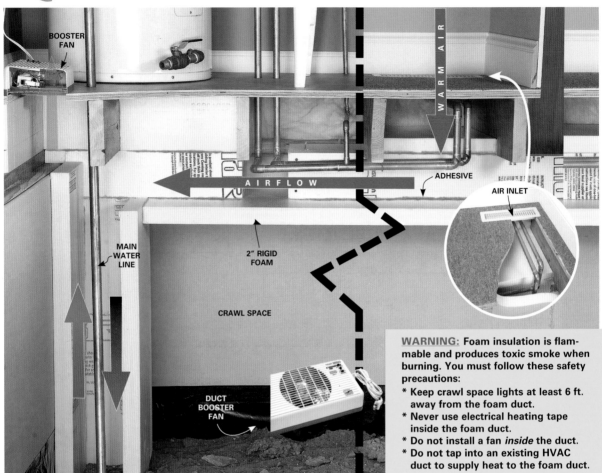

BOOSTER FAN

WARM AIR

AIRFLOW

ADHESIVE

AIR INLET

MAIN WATER LINE

2" RIGID FOAM

CRAWL SPACE

DUCT BOOSTER FAN

WARNING: Foam insulation is flammable and produces toxic smoke when burning. You must follow these safety precautions:
* **Keep crawl space lights at least 6 ft. away from the foam duct.**
* **Never use electrical heating tape inside the foam duct.**
* **Do not install a fan *inside* the duct.**
* **Do not tap into an existing HVAC duct to supply heat to the foam duct.**

PREVENT PIPES FROM FREEZING

I insulated the heating ducts in my crawl space and my pipes froze. I can't insulate the walls of the crawl space because it's vented to the outside. How can I insulate the pipes to keep them from freezing?

For starters, forget about using fiberglass or the foam pipe insulation sold at home centers. At best, it provides an insulation value of R-3.8. That's not enough to prevent frozen pipes during extended cold periods. Plus it's difficult to install on existing pipes, especially when the pipes run along the length of a floor joist. So we put our heads together and came up with a solution that we're all but positive will work for you. One of the editors used this fix to successfully insulate freeze-prone pipes on an outside wall.

Here's how it works. Build a duct system around the pipes with 2-in.-thick rigid extruded polystyrene foam (R-10). It works by drawing heated household air through the foam duct and back into the house. Start by locat-

ing a spot near the pipes on one end of the crawl space near a wall and cut a 5 x 10-in. hole in the floor above. This exhaust hole should be near an electrical outlet. Cut another hole at the far end of the pipes to fit a conventional floor vent—the size is up to you.

Next construct the duct by running the foam down a few inches below the pipes to create enough room for airflow. Glue the lengths together with PL-300 blue construction adhesive and pin them with screws or nails until the adhesive sets up. Crosscut individual foam pieces to "cap off" any open joist areas. Cutting is easy with a circular or table saw.

Use the same method to encase vertical riser pipes and pipes that run along the length of a joist. Once all pipes are enclosed, glue on end caps.

Buy a duct booster fan (available in the HVAC department at home centers for $34) and place it over the exhaust vent. Run the fan full time at low speed during freezing weather (that'll cost about $3 per month).

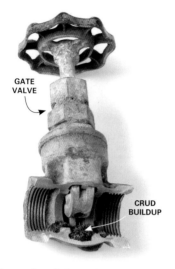

GATE VALVE

CRUD BUILDUP

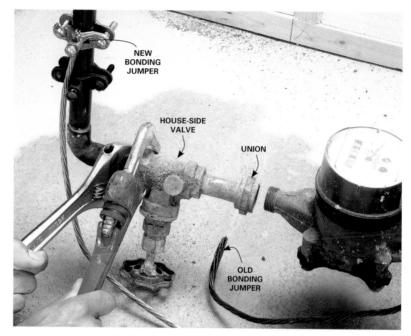

NEW BONDING JUMPER

HOUSE-SIDE VALVE

UNION

OLD BONDING JUMPER

1 Shut off the street-side valve where the water enters the house. Then loosen the coupling nut and remove the nipple from the old valve.

NEW BALL VALVE

LEATHER WASHER

2 Screw on the new ball valve, install the old nipple and the new leather washer (use Teflon tape or pipe dope on the threads). Tighten the coupling nut, turn on the water and check for leaks.

Every time I do a plumbing job at my house, I crank the main shut-off valve down as tight as I can get it, but water still drips out of the open pipe. Can I replace the main valve myself?

Sure, but you have to get your ducks in a row before you start. To remove the old valve, you'll have to undo the coupling on the "house side" of the water meter. There's usually an oil-impregnated leather sealing washer inside the coupling. Leather washers are tough to find, so look at a plumbing supplier or buy them from Twin Leather Co., twinleather.com; 508-583-3485. (Its "home washer repair kit" contains two 5/8-in. and two 3/4-in. leather washers and costs $5 plus shipping.) Some plumbing suppliers sell neoprene washers, but the "old-timers" swear by leather, because eventually neoprene will dry out and crack. You probably have a 3/4-in. pipe leading to and from the leaky valve. Buy a threaded replacement ball valve; it's a far better choice than the older gate-style valve.

Test the "street-side" valve where the water enters the house. Since that valve is just as old, test it to make sure it closes all the way and reopens again. If that valve needs replacement, contact your water utility to shut off the main valve at the curb.

Then check out the electrical system "bonding jumper" that runs from a clamp on the house side of the meter to a clamp on the street side. If you can unscrew the old valve with the bonding jumper wire in place, fine. If you can't, do not disconnect it. The safe way to work around this problem is to install a longer section of copper wire and two new clamps (6AWG for 100-amp service, 4AWG for 200-amp service). Then remove the short bonding jumper. At that point, you're ready to shut down the water and replace the valve as shown.

Question& Answer

FIX ROTTING A/C INSULATION

The black foam on one of my outside A/C lines is rotting and falling off. I suspect it's costing me money because the cold tubing is always covered with condensation. Is this something to worry about?

You're right—that condensation is reducing the efficiency of your A/C and raising your energy costs. You should remove all the old foam insulation and install the correct foam. Unfortunately, you won't find it at any home center. Measure the outside diameter on the larger of the two tubes (the skinny tube doesn't need insulation). Then contact a refrigeration supply house or online supplier for new foam and insulating tape (Insul-Lock tubing insulating foam, $4 for 6-ft. lengths, and Nomaco Poly Tape, $5, both from pexsupply.com).

1 Seal the ends. Wipe off the condensation and wrap a few winds of the sticky poly tape on the tubing where it exits the house. Then dry and wrap the service valve on the condenser end of the tubing. Squeeze it in tight around the tubing.

2 Install new foam. Slip the new foam over the tubing and on top of the cork tape. Remove the adhesive liner, align the edges and press the seam together as you go. Be careful. Once the glued ends touch, you can't get them apart again.

KEEPING COLD BREWS IN THE GARAGE

We got a new refrigerator and put the old side-by-side in the garage. The food in the fridge side stays cool, but the freezer doesn't keep the food frozen in cold weather. What gives?

Most refrigerators use a single compressor to cool the freezer and the cold-food compartment. Unfortunately, there's only one thermostat and it's inside the cold-food section. So if the temperature in the garage stays about 38° F, the thermostat never turns on. The cold air chills the food in the refrigerator, but it's not cold enough to keep frozen food solid (the ideal freezer temperature is 0° F).

You may be able to solve your problem by installing a "garage kit," a heating coil to warm the air around the thermostat. The warmer air makes the compressor run longer and keeps frozen food, well, frozen. Check with the manufacturer to see if it makes one for your model.

But before you shell out $20 for the kit, consider how much you'll have to spend to keep your brews chilled and pizzas frozen in the summer. Your old fridge is less efficient than your new one, so it's already costing you more to run. Add 25 percent to run the old clunker in an 80-degree garage. Then double the bill if it's running in a garage at 90 degrees and up. Are you sure you want to pay that much just to save a trip to the kitchen?

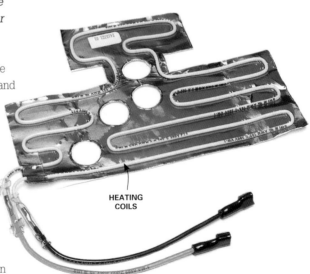

Find the model number of your refrigerator and contact the manufacturer's parts department to see if it offers a garage kit for your unit. This one costs $20.

WATER HEATER PUDDLE? REPLACE THE TPR VALVE

Lately I'm seeing a puddle of water on the floor next to the water heater. The drain valve isn't leaking and I can't find a leak in the pipes. What's going on?

If you've had the heater for a long time and the problem just started, chances are the temperature pressure relief (TPR) valve is bad. The TPR is a safety device that releases water pressure when it becomes dangerously high within the water heater. But before you run out and buy a new TPR valve, check with your local water utility to see if it has made any changes to the system that would boost water pressure. If not, go ahead and replace the valve (less than $10 at a home center). Shut off the gas valve or flip the breaker to your water heater. Wait three hours for it to cool down or run the hot water until it's lukewarm. Then shut off the water and bleed the pressure by opening a hot water faucet near the heater.

If a new valve doesn't solve the problem, it's time to install an expansion tank (about $40 at home centers). The tank has an internal air bladder that acts like a shock absorber to prevent overpressure in the system. Consult the chart at the home center for proper tank sizing. Install the tank on the cold water line and support the line with metal strapping (**photo below**).

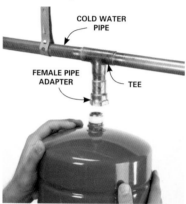

IF THE NEW VALVE LEAKS, ADD AN EXPANSION TANK
If a new TPR valve didn't solve the problem, solder in a "tee" and a female-threaded fitting on a horizontal cold water line near the water heater. Then wrap the tank threads with Teflon tape and screw in the tank. NOTE: Toss the saddle tee that comes with the expansion tank and install a tee and threaded fitting instead. Saddle tees always leak over time.

FIRST, REPLACE THE TPR VALVE
Cut the overflow tube on a top-mount TPR with a hacksaw. Then unscrew the threaded fitting from the old TPR valve and install the new valve. Reattach the overflow tube by soldering in a coupler, or use a push-on connector.

GreatGoofs®

Nuts and bolts of washers

When my washing machine suddenly started smoking (the motor, I mean!), I turned it off, pulled the back access panel free and checked the motor. It stank like burned motor windings, but everything else looked fine. Instead of springing for a new washer, I replaced the motor. Everything seemed to be working again, giving me a fine feeling of another DIY conquest. But 10 minutes into the next load, the motor burned out a second time.

At that point, I decided to buy a new machine. After setting aside the old one and wrestling the new unit downstairs and hooking it up, I moved the clothes from the broken washer to the new one. As I pulled out the last pair of blue jeans, I noticed a 3-in. nail that had fallen through a hole in the drum and kept the motor from turning. Now I have two perfectly good washers and one good motor. Oh, well. I'm not the first person to ruin something with an errant nail.

Question& Answer

HOW TIGHT IS HAND-TIGHT?

The directions that came with the toilet supply line said to hand-tighten the connectors. Then the connection leaked. So I used pliers to crank it down. It turned almost two full turns. Did I overdo it?

If it were up to us, no manufacturer would be allowed to use cheap plastic compression nuts on supply lines. Your question is one we hear often. In fact, Max Lemberger, one of our field editors, just told us his toilet tale of woe. Hand-tightening caused a leak and pliers-tightening caused the compression nut to crack—days after he installed the supply line. The result was a small flood.

Here's our official advice: Buy a supply line that has a metal nut or a reinforced plastic compression nut. If you can't find one, tighten the regular plastic nut in two stages. First tighten it enough to stop the water from leaking. Then come back a few hours later (when the rubber gasket has compressed a bit) and snug it up a tad more. Never crank on a plastic nut with pliers.

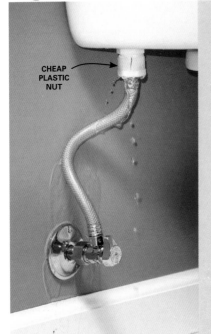

CHEAP PLASTIC NUT

REINFORCING RIBS

Buy a supply line that has a metal nut or a reinforced plastic nut.

WHOLE LOT OF SHAKIN' GOIN' ON

DAMPENER PADS

Clean the floor under the pads. Then stick the adhesive discs to the floor. Apply the primer to the pads and press them onto the discs. Lift the washer back into place, locating the feet in the pad recesses.

PRIMER

ADHESIVE DISC

I've leveled my front-loading washer, but it still vibrates like crazy. I'm thinking about bolting it to the floor.

Whoa! That'll just make more noise. Instead of connecting the washer to the floor, you want to isolate it from the floor. The washer's rubber feet are supposed to do that. Unfortunately, at high spin speeds, they don't do a very good job.

That's where vibration isolation/dampening pads come in. Installers use these heavy-duty rubber pads under furnaces and blowers. One company makes a pad specifically for front-loading washing machines. The puck-shaped pads made by Good Vibrations Inc. (330-606-0978) get good reviews. You can get a set of four for $47 plus shipping from gviinc.net.

Installing the pads is a three-step process, and you'll need a helper for lifting the machine. Start by lifting each corner of the machine and slipping a pad under each foot. Mark each pad location on the floor. Then lift the washer out of the way so you can apply the adhesive discs and mount the pads to the floor as shown.

SAVE MONEY ON YOUR WATER BILL

I'm on city water and sewer and my bill keeps climbing. I'm thinking of replacing the water-gulping appliances. Which will pay off the most?

Buying appliances that are more water efficient is one of the last places to start cutting water usage. The No. 1 cause of a rising water/sewer bill is a leak somewhere in the house (10 percent of all homes have a leak of at least 90 gallons per day). And the No. 1 culprit is a running toilet. Toilet parts usually start leaking slowly and get worse over time. So by the time you notice it, months may have passed. When you consider that a leaking toilet can cost you almost $45 per month for water and sewer, it makes sense to fix any leaky toilets in your house before anything else.

Leaking flappers and deteriorated beveled washers are the most common failure points. The parts are cheap (less than $5), so the payback is enormous. Replace them all annually to eliminate a very real water-wasting potential leak.

Even if your toilet isn't leaking, it's probably still wasting water. Consider these water-wasting facts: If your house was built before 1980, the original toilet is wasting $170 every year. If it's newer (1980–1994), it's wasting $99

a year. A new WaterSense–rated toilet costs as little as $100. So that's the fixture to replace first because the payback is huge! Some utilities are even offering rebates to sweeten the deal. Visit epa.gov/watersense/rebate_finder_saving_money_water.html to find rebates in your area.

Next on the fast payback list is a water-saving showerhead. Many older (pre-1992) showerheads had a flow rate of as much as 5.5 gallons per minute. A WaterSense–rated head must use no more than 2.0 gpm. But you can buy super-efficient showerheads that provide a vigorous shower using only 1.5 gpm. The Oxygenics 630-XLF15 is one model ($26 from faucetdepot.com). The showerhead sucks in air from around the spray nozzle and uses it to pressurize the shower stream. The water and energy savings make this a one-month payback.

Few know this, but you pay twice for water—once when it enters your house and again when it goes down the sewer. The water meter doesn't know that the water you use for irrigating never goes down the sewer. Ask your water/sewer utility if it has a "deduct" program for

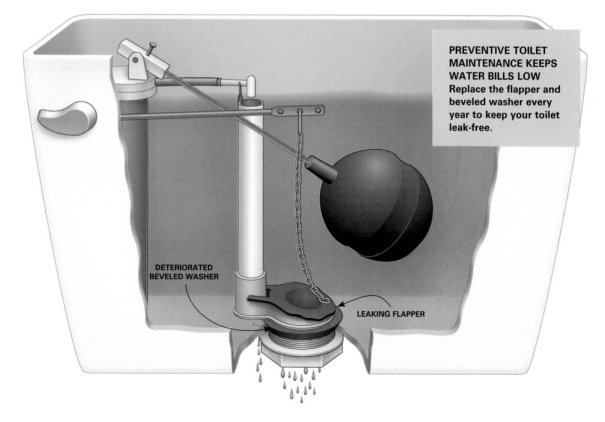

PREVENTIVE TOILET MAINTENANCE KEEPS WATER BILLS LOW
Replace the flapper and beveled washer every year to keep your toilet leak-free.

DETERIORATED BEVELED WASHER

LEAKING FLAPPER

lawn sprinkling. If so, you can track the amount of water you use for irrigation and deduct that volume from your sewer bill. You'll still have to pay for the water. But since it doesn't go down the drain, it can save you a bundle on the sewer portion of the bill. Of course, you'll have to replumb your hose bibs and water sprinkler system through a separate meter to prove your deduction. But water meters are cheap (the meter shown, far right, the WM75, cost $77 at assuredautomation.com/WM).

I purposely left out new front-loading clothes washers, even though they use half the water of older top-loaders. They're a great choice if you're in the market for a new washer. But don't buy a new efficient washer until you've replaced your toilets and showerheads. The payback on a front-loading washer is a lengthy 5.8 years.

AIR IN

POWERFUL SHOWER STREAM

OXYGENICS

ASSUREDAUTOMATION.COM

GET A VIGOROUS SHOWER WITH LESS WATER
Twist off your old water-wasting showerhead and spin on a super-efficient 1.5 gpm model. It sucks air into the head to build volume and pressure.

SAVE ON THE SEWER BILL
Water meters are a bit of work to install, but they can track the amount of water you use for irrigation to help you save on your sewer bill.

GreatGoofs®

Out-the-window AC

Last fall we wanted to remove the air conditioner from a second-floor window for the winter. Instead of waiting for my husband to do it, my son and I figured we could handle the job ourselves. We removed the screws and tried to open the window, but it wouldn't budge. So we looked for more screws and pounded on the window sash to make sure it wasn't stuck. No dice.

I told my son to step back as I pried up on the window sash with a big crowbar. The window shot open and the now unfettered AC unit tipped out of the opening, bounced down the entry roof, flew over the gutter, and smashed into several pieces on the ground. I guess I should have waited for my husband's help after all.

HOT ROOM?

Six ways to cool it off!

Do you have a room in your house that swelters all summer long? Most people immediately think of a window air conditioner. That can be a smart solution, but it doesn't work in every case, and it isn't the only option. Check out these six cool alternatives. One of them might be the perfect solution for your hot and sticky problem.

HOT AIR EXITS
THROUGH ATTIC
VENTS

PAUL PERREAULT
(BAKED MEDIA)

PLUMBING, HEATING & APPLIANCES

1. Cool down with a whole-house fan

Whole-house fans may seem old fashioned, but they're enjoying renewed popularity. The idea behind them is simple. A powerful fan draws cooler early morning and evening air through open doors and windows and forces it up through the attic and out the roof vents. This sends hot air up and out, cooling your house and your attic. These fans are commonly mounted in an upstairs stairwell or hallway ceiling where there's at least 3 ft. of clearance above the fan.

Main advantages

- Energy savings. They use 90 percent less energy than an air conditioner, and in dry climates with cool mornings and evenings, they can actually replace your AC system.
- Easy installation. With a helper and basic tools, you can install a whole-house fan in a weekend.

Main disadvantages

- They can't cool inside temps any lower than outside temps, and they can't dehumidify.
- They can make allergies worse. Whole-house fans draw in outdoor pollen and dust.

- Larger fans move air quickly, but they cost more to purchase and install. They also require significant attic ventilation and make more noise than smaller attic fans.

For the best results, match the fan size to your floor plan, cooling needs and available attic ventilation. Call your local utility and check energy-star.gov to see which models qualify for local rebates and any possible federal tax credits. Fans cost $200 to $1,200.

**tamtech.com,
quietcoolfan.com,
airvent.com**

A whole-house fan uses one-tenth as much power as AC. It draws cooler outside air in through open doors and windows to create a pleasant breeze that pushes hot air out through attic vents.

R-38–INSULATED
SEALED DOORS

Newer attic fans have insulated doors that close in 30 seconds when the fan's not operating.

REMOTE
CONTROL KIT

TAMTECH

2. Portable air conditioner lets you chill

Portable air conditioners are similar to window units in operation. They sit on the floor (on casters) and use an adapter kit to vent the hot air through a hose running through a window, a wall or a sliding glass door.

Main advantages

- They are easy to install and use.
- You can move them from room to room.

Main disadvantages

- They're almost twice as expensive and use more

energy than a similar-size window unit with the same cooling capacity.
- At this time there are no Energy Star–qualified portable room air conditioners.

Portables range in price from $300 to $1,500 depending on the size, features and efficiency.

**friedrich.com, sharpusa.com,
sylvane.com**

FRIEDRICH

Portable air conditioners are an alternative to a window unit. They're easy to operate and to move from room to room. However, they cost more and use more energy.

3. Mini-split system is cool and quiet

Long popular in Europe and Japan, a mini-split system air conditioner (sometimes called ductless AC), is a hybrid of central air and a window unit. A small condenser sits outside and connects through a conduit to an inside evaporator mounted high on the wall or ceiling.

Main advantages

- Silent operation. The condenser sits outside, it doesn't let in street noise and the indoor fan is whisper quiet.
- The system can be mounted anywhere thanks to the small size of the indoor and outdoor components. The conduit, which houses the power cable, refrigerant tubing, suction tubing and a condensate drain, runs through a 3-in. hole hidden behind the indoor evaporator.
- Zoning flexibility lets you cool rooms individually.

Main disadvantage

- Cost. Professional installation costs $1,500 to $2,500 including parts and labor. You can install it yourself, but it's fairly complicated and you'll most likely void the manufacturer's warranty. Systems with an efficiency rating of 16 or higher may qualify for a federal tax credit.

Sources: mrslim.com, friedrich.com, lge.com

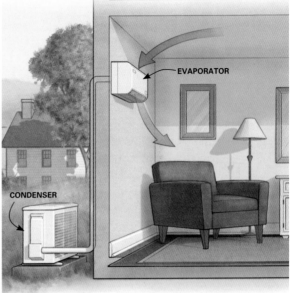

Mini-split AC systems don't require ductwork and can be run to one or more rooms. Their small size, quiet operation and individual zoning let you cool only the room you're using, which can save energy and money.

---

4. In-wall AC unit stays put all year

An in-wall air conditioner is basically the same as a window unit. The primary difference is that it has vents on the back instead of along the sides and it sits flush or extends only slightly farther out from the exterior wall.

Main advantages

- Permanent installation means you don't have to lug it in and out twice a year, and it's not an easy entry point for burglars.
- It doesn't block a window.
- The chassis unit sits securely inside a metal sleeve that is installed into the wall. The chassis unit slides out for easy servicing.
- The size of the unit isn't limited to a standard window opening, so it can be bigger and more powerful than a window unit.

Main disadvantages

- Installation is more involved. Cutting a hole in the outside wall of your home may be difficult depending on the exterior sheathing of your home.
- You may need to install a new electrical circuit. Some larger units require 240 volts (although most smaller units can be plugged into a standard 120-volt outlet). Energy Star–qualified models use 25 percent less

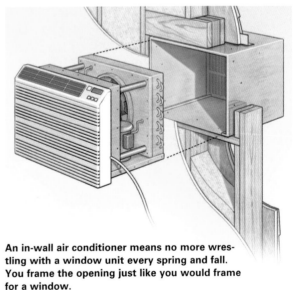

An in-wall air conditioner means no more wrestling with a window unit every spring and fall. You frame the opening just like you would frame for a window.

energy than models made before late 2000. Check with your utility for energy rebates. Some units provide both cooling and heating. Prices range from $400 for cooling a 400- to 700-sq.-ft. room to $700 or so for cooling/heating a 1,000-sq.-ft. space.

friedrich.com, lennox.com, geappliances.com

5. Move the cool air with a ventilator fan

If you have a hot room in an otherwise comfortable house, you can pump existing cool air into that hot room using a special fan installed in the wall or floor.

Main advantages

■ No extra cooling costs. The Aireshare level-to-level ventilator fan (shown) moves existing cool air from one level (from the basement or a mini-split system, for example) to another level of the house through an adjustable sleeve installed through the floor/ceiling.

■ A ventilator fan can blow conditioned air up or down, depending on the position of the blower unit. There are also room-to-room ventilator fans to move the conditioned air.

Main disadvantages

■ To install the fan, you'll have to cut a hole through the floor/ceiling and run an electrical line to the unit.

■ It's only practical if you have an abundance of existing cool air that's easily accessible to your hot room. Level-to-level ventilator fans (about $190) can also be

A ventilator fan can move existing cool air from one level or room to another through the wall or floor.

COOL AIR FROM
LOWER LEVEL

JOHN HARTMAN

used to move warm air through the living space during the winter. Search online for "level-to-level fan."

tjernlund.com, aftproducts.com

---

6. Increase the flow with a duct or a vent booster fan

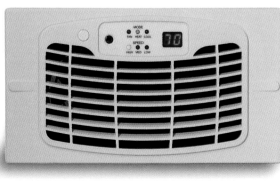

TJERNLUND

In-line duct (top) and vent booster fans (below) increase the flow of cool air through ducts and registers.

AIRFLOW TECHNOLOGY

If you have forced-air cooling but there's still a room that's hotter than all the rest, a duct or vent booster fan can increase the flow of cool air into that room. Two types of booster fans are available.

An in-line duct booster fan fits inside the duct of the room you're trying to cool. You mount the fan near the outlet and it automatically kicks on when your cooling system runs.

Vent and register booster fans sit directly on top of or replace ceiling, floor or wall registers. Depending on the model, you can set it to operate automatically, control it with a switch or operate it by a remote control.

Main advantages

■ Easy to install and use.

■ Reasonably priced. In-line duct booster fans are available in both plug-in and hard-wired models and retail for $30 to $150. Vent and register booster units plug into a nearby electrical outlet or can be hard-wired. Register and vent duct booster fans cost $40 to $100.

Main disadvantages

■ Less powerful (and cheaper) in-line units have a lighter-gauge housing that is more prone to rattling.

■ Duct or vent booster fans may not make a significant cooling difference if your ductwork or overall cooling system is inefficient, sized improperly or faulty.

Search online for "in-line duct booster fan" or "register duct booster fan" to find dealers. (These fans can also be used to increase the flow of warm air through ducts during the winter months.

Tools & Skills

MAGNET

TAPE MEASURE CLIP

QUICK-DRAW MEASURING TAPE

The clip on my measuring tape used to fray the pockets on my jeans. Here's my solution. I unscrewed the clip from the tape and screwed on a pot magnet in its place. I hook the clip onto my pocket and stick the magnetized tape to it. The clip stays in my pocket all day, and the magnet makes it easy to grab the tape and put it back when I'm done.

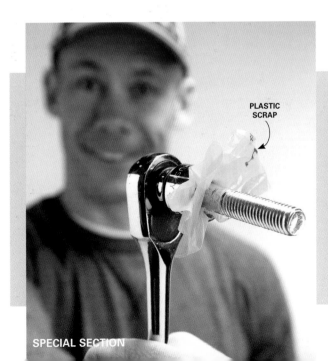

PLASTIC SCRAP

SOCKET WRENCH HINT

When you're using a socket wrench to ratchet on a bolt in a spot where your fingers can't reach, how do you get it started? Simple. Stick a little piece of plastic bag between the bolt head and the socket. The thickness of the plastic will hold the bolt tight until you get it in place, and the plastic will fall right off when you take the socket off the bolt.

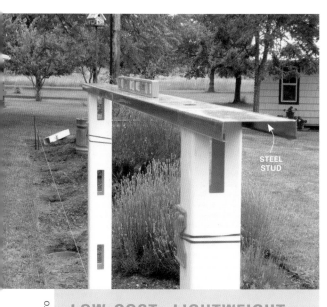

LOW-COST, LIGHTWEIGHT 8-FT. LEVEL

A good 8-ft. level can cost almost $200, but you can make a good substitute with a steel stud and a 2- or 4-ft. level. Unlike wood, steel studs are always straight and weigh almost nothing. And if your level is magnetic, you can stick it to the stud for vertical work.

STEEL STUD

EASY-FIND SCREWDRIVERS

Although I have a bunch of screwdrivers, I can never seem to find the one I need. Here's a way to help identify your screwdrivers at a glance. Use a permanent marker to label their size and type on the handle. I use an "X" for a Phillips head and a dash for a flathead.

CLOG-FREE BELT SANDING

Last spring, I was cleaning some new treated deck boards with my belt sander to prep the wood for a semitransparent stain. All the gunk on the boards kept clogging up the belt. To keep the belt clean and make it last longer, I screwed a wire brush to the sawhorse and every so often touched the running belt to the brush. It cleaned the belt up nicely—and my new deck looks great!

Tools & Skills

SIMPLER SKIM-COATING

A new approach that's easy to master

If you're a skilled drywall taper or plasterer, you probably use a hawk and trowel to skim-coat walls. We don't expect to change your mind if you use those tools as second hands. But if you're a remodeler who does only occasional skim-coating to fix wrecked walls, you know it's a tough skill to master.

The method we show isn't faster than traditional skim-coating—you have to do two or three coats and let each one dry in-between. But it's idiot-proof, and the walls will end up flat and smooth. So if you're a contractor who's given up on skim-coating and you always call in a taper for the task, you can save on labor by tackling it yourself next time. It only takes a regular paint roller and a squeegee knife. The 14-in.-wide squeegee knife we used is called a Magic Trowel. It costs $25. To find online sources, search for "TexMaster 9927" or "squeegee knife."

Start by prepping the walls

With this method, you don't just spot-prime; you roll the entire wall with a stain-blocking sealer (**Photo 1**). If you've always used solvent-based sealers like traditional BIN and KILZ, it's time to try one of the water-based stain killers. Water-based BIN works well, and you won't have to worry about the smell. But don't rush on to the next step; let the sealer dry thoroughly before applying any joint compound.

These are thin layers that won't fix holes or torn-away paper, or make uneven sections level. Patch these problems with setting-type joint compound. Let the compound harden (it doesn't have to be dry) before you start skim-coating.

Roll on the mud

Mix all-purpose joint compound to about the same consistency as mud you'd use for bedding tape (the consistency of mayonnaise, or just thin enough to roll on the wall). You'll get shrinkage if you mix it too wet. Don't worry if you get cracking on the first coat; just mix the

STAIN-SEALING PRIMER

1 Prime the walls. Roll a fast-drying, stain-sealing primer on the walls. The primer seals loose paper and promotes better adhesion of the joint compound.

THINNED JOINT COMPOUND

2 Roll on the mud. Spread a layer of slightly thinned all-purpose joint compound on the walls with a heavy-nap roller. Work in small sections so you can smooth out the joint compound before it starts to dry.

next coat a little thicker by spooning in some fresh mud from another bucket.

Use a 1/2-in.-nap roller to roll mud on an area about 4 ft. square (**Photo 2**). Try to keep it as even as you can so the squeegee work will go better for you.

Wipe it smooth

Smooth the mud with the squeegee knife. Keep a damp rag and a mud pan handy. Use the rag to wipe the blade after every few strokes and the mud pan to wipe off excess mud that builds up on the blade. Starting at the top corner, set the squeegee knife against the wall and pull it down (**Photo 3**). Overlap each vertical pass until you finish the section. You may have to go over some areas a few times. It won't take you long to get the hang of using the squeegee knife.

Tip

Give this squeegee-like taping knife a shot for smoothing out tape joints next time you tape. It tapers the edges and you'll have no trowel or taping knife marks.

When you're done with the top section, roll joint compound on the lower half. Pull the squeegee knife from the bottom up (**Photo 4**). Touch up along the edges as you go.

Let the first coat of joint compound dry. To speed up drying time, especially if the air is humid, use a space heater and a box fan or two. You don't have to sand between coats; just knock off lumps or proud mud lines with a 5- or 6-in. putty knife to avoid streaks in the next coat (**Photo 5**).

Apply one or two more layers

It sounds like a lot of work to apply two or three coats of joint compound, but the process is quick and the thin layers dry fast. As you know, the smoother you get the wall, the less sanding you'll have to tackle. Trowel off each successive layer at a right angle to the previous one. After the last coat dries, pole-sand the wall with 120-grit paper. If you have too many peaks and valleys, hit the walls with 100-grit first.

4 Pull up from the bottom. **Roll joint compound onto the lower section and smooth it by pulling the trowel upward.**

3 Trowel the first coat. **Smooth the joint compound with the squeegee knife. Start in the top corner and pull down.**

SQUEEGEE KNIFE

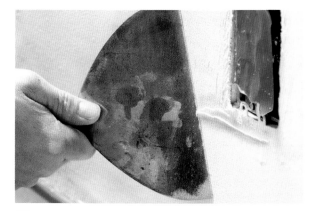

5 Scrape off lumps. **Scrape the wall with a 6-in. putty knife to remove lumps and ridges. Brush off the wall and you're ready for the next coat.**

6 Change directions for the second coat. **Trowel the second coat horizontally. If you still see indentations or imperfections after the second coat dries, trowel on a third coat.**

Tools & Skills: Shop Rat

ROUTER LIFTS

If you've seen those slick router lifts in catalogs and wondered whether they're worth the painful price, here's my take: I used to have an under-mounted plunge router on an oversize plastic base, and it was a royal pain in the butt. I'd have to either extract the beast to make fine depth adjustments or crawl under the table like a reptile. Neither option was fun and both required several tries to get the depth set just right. And there was also the hassle of changing bits.

Then I got a router lift, and I love it. It makes extremely fine height adjustments simple and fast just by turning a crank. My Jessem model cost about $300, and the dedicated Porter Cable router cost another $300. There are $200 ones on the market, but I haven't given them a try. If you do lots of routing on router tables, a router lift is well worth the big bucks.

WORKBENCH POWER STRIP

Screw a power strip to the side of your workbench and you won't have to monkey with extension cords anymore when using power tools for bench work.

DOUBLE YOUR BATTERY LIFE

Here's a tip for making lithium tool batteries last twice as long. Most kits come with two batteries. Take one of them and stick it in the refrigerator—with the milk, not the ice cream. Lithium-ion batteries have a shelf life of only a few years even if you use them sparingly. And new batteries are expensive. But keeping one cold makes it last at least twice as long. Granted, you'll be a little inconvenienced from time to time waiting for a dead battery to recharge, so this tip won't be practical for pros.

When the first battery finally gives up the ghost, you can start all over with a practically brand new one. And by the way, frequent full discharges will wear out your battery quicker. Several partial discharges with short recharges are better than running the battery dead and then giving it a complete refill.

A WHEEL-Y PORTABLE COMPRESSOR!

Some small air compressors are about as portable as an engine block with a suitcase handle. But Sheldon Buda fixed that: He replaced the rubber feet with casters, and now his compressor rolls around like a shop vacuum. You may have to drill out the mounting holes a bit to fit the caster shafts and shorten the shafts with a hacksaw, but it's worth it.

SAVE BIG BUCKS ON TOOLS

Editor Gary Wentz loves two things: power tools and saving a buck. If Dumpster diving were an Olympic event, I'd want him on our team. Naturally, you won't find a guy like him at the home center paying full freight for tools—no, sir! Gary goes online and buys factory-reconditioned tools and, according to him, he hasn't been stung yet. Some have been returned because of a mechanical problem or just a dent in the case. Whatever their histories, the tools have been inspected, tested and repaired, if necessary. Most are covered by the same warranty as a brand-new tool.

Gary has bought at least a dozen tools in the last few years, and all have performed flawlessly. Here are his shopping tips. First find out the cost of new before you buy. Though savings are 10 to 40 percent, you may only save $10 and wind up spending more than that on shipping. Second, if you find a bargain, grab it. Supplies of any specific model are limited. To find the tool you want, go online and search for "reconditioned tools."

This reconditioned jigsaw was $70 less than a brand-new one.

Tools & Skills: Shop Rat

HOMEMADE BENCH PUCKS

Rockler sells ingenious little things called Bench Cookies for $12 for a set of four (rockler.com; 800-279-4441). Not a bad price, I'd say. They're very useful when you need to space projects above the workbench for clamping, finishing or routing. But if you need lots of them, or you love saving a few bucks, you can buy hockey pucks for about $1.25 each and stick shelf liner on both sides with spray adhesive.

T-BAR ASSEMBLY LIFTS

Ever wonder what makes a woodworker tick? Here's Ken Collier, the editor in chief: "These T-bars are one of my happiest discoveries as a woodworker. They're just 5-in.-wide pieces of 3/4-in. plywood face-glued together, with another 5-in. piece screwed on the bottom for a base. Any larger assembly I do happens on the T-bars because they lift it off the table. It's easy to drive in screws, check the project for square-ness and tighten clamps anywhere around the edges. I work alone most of the time, and the T-bars are my extra set of hands."

EASY-OFF SANDING SLEEVES

I couldn't live without my spindle sander for super-smooth sanding of inside curves on projects, but for years I dreaded chang-ing spindle sizes. That's because it was difficult to tighten the bolt enough to expand the rubber drum, so the sanding sleeve often slid up and down the drum while I was sanding. And if I managed to tight-en up the bolt enough, it was nearly impossible to loosen it again. Last week, a hand screw miraculously jumped onto the sander table and solved the prob-lem. I tightened it around the drum and easily twist-ed the bolt. Hallelujah!

MIKE KRIVIT

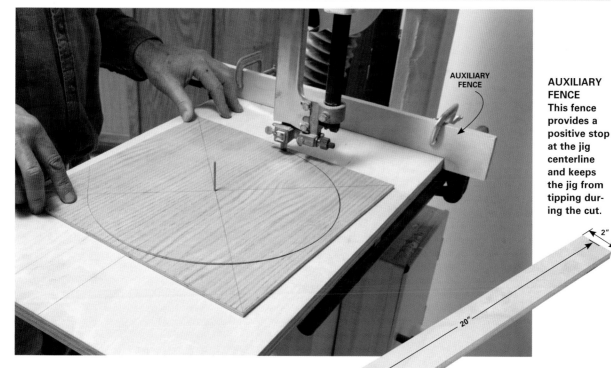

AUXILIARY FENCE

AUXILIARY FENCE This fence provides a positive stop at the jig centerline and keeps the jig from tipping during the cut.

Cutting perfect circles is easy with a band saw—as long as you take a half hour to build yourself a cutting jig. I've cut circles with radiuses ranging from a few inches to a couple of feet. The only limit is the distance from the fence to the saw blade.

Use any 3/4-in. plywood to make the jig, and attach a runner to the underside that fits in the band saw's miter gauge slot. That will hold everything steady while you turn the actual circle stock through the blade. Then make yourself an auxiliary fence from another piece of 3/4-in. plywood as shown. Send the jig through the blade to create the saw kerf, then shut off the saw when the blade reaches the centerline and lock the fence about 1/8 in.

away from the jig. Clamp the auxiliary fence to the band saw fence with the stop against the edge of the jig. Hold it slightly above the jig so the jig will slide easily beneath it. The auxiliary fence not only stops the jig at the right spot for turning circles but also keeps the jig from tipping up from the band saw table.

Cutting is simple. You'll need to choose narrow blades for small circles. Push the jig with the mounted cutting blank until you reach the stop and then just twist the blank through the blade. You'll have a small amount of cleanup to do where the cut starts and stops. You're done.

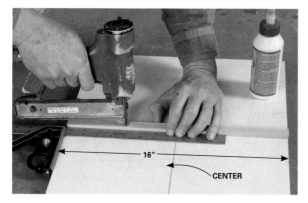

1 Attach the runner. **Cut 3/4-in. plywood to 16 x 24 in. Draw centerlines on both sides, then glue and pin the runner to the bottom. Send the jig through the blade until you reach the centerline, then clamp the auxiliary fence to the jigsaw fence.**

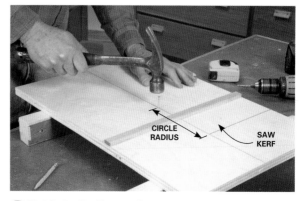

2 Finish the jig. **Tap a nail through the hole, then flip the jig over. Drill a hole in the middle of the blank and prop the circle stock over the nail shank.**

SPECIAL SECTION
TOOLS & SKILLS

Tools&Skills: **Shop Rat**

DRILL PRESS TABLE

Drill presses are designed for working with metal, not wood. That's why, 10 years ago, I screwed an old scrap of 3/4-in. treated plywood to the metal table so I could screw down or clamp stops and fences. Frankly, I was embarrassed by it and finally built this dedicated woodworking drill press table. Mine is a bit over the top, with dadoes, plastic laminate and T-Tracks. Tackle it if you wish. The truth is, you could make a quick and easy top by bolting two glued layers of particleboard to the cast-iron table from the underside. You can screw or clamp temporary stops and fences to that and have a serviceable table. But your table won't be as fetching or as easy to use as mine.

Here's an overview of the construction process. Glue 1-in. oversized particleboard panels together, then cut them to size on the table saw. Edge-band both sides of the table, then belt-sand the top so the hardwood is flush with the surfaces. Cut the laminate squares 1 in. oversize and apply them with contact

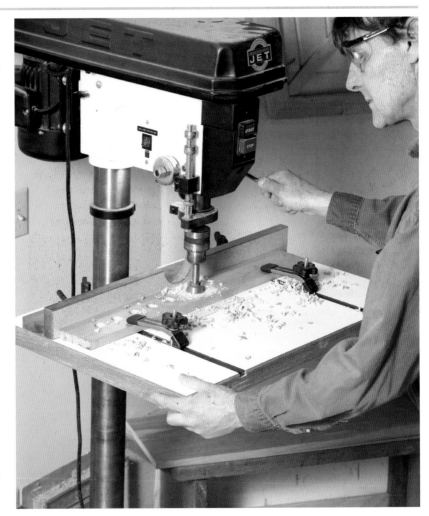

Bells and whistles

FENCE: A semicircular clearance hole for the chuck allows for drilling holes that are close to the fence.

THROAT PLATE: An inset 1/2-in. replaceable throat plate takes the abuse so the top does not.

T-TRACKS: T-Tracks are universally useful gizmos that allow you to endlessly adjust jigs, fences and hold-downs. On this table, they're used for a sliding fence and hold-downs.

LAMINATE: Plastic laminate on both the top and bottom will keep the top from warping with humidity changes.

EDGING: A hardwood edge-banding protects the rather delicate core from getting dinged up—plus, it's pretty.

cement. Then rout the laminate squares flush with a flush-trim bit and chamfer them with a 45-degree bit. Rout out the 1/2-in.-deep recess for the throat plate.

Cut the 3/4-in.-wide dadoes on the table saw. Cut the clearance hole on the fence with a 2-1/2-in. hole saw on the drill press. Screw the fence together before applying the laminate, then rout that as you did with the tabletop.

Lag screws (1-1/2 x 5/16 in.) and washers work great for securing your new top to the existing drill press table. The instructions with the T-Track will tell you the rest.

PLASTIC LAMINATE

3"

1x3

45° BEVEL

1/2" x 4-1/2" x 4-1/2"

3/8" x 3/4" DADOES

PLASTIC LAMINATE

45° BEVEL

1/2" RECESS

T-TRACK

20"

30"

PARTICLEBOARD (TWO LAYERS)

1x2 HARDWOOD

Figure A
Drill press table

SHOPPING LIST

Table: Two 2-ft. squares of particleboard. (You can get 2x2s at most home centers or have them cut them from full sheets.)

Edge band: 8 lin. ft. of 1x2 hardwood.

Fence: 6 lin. ft. of 1x3 hardwood.

Laminate: Buy the smallest size sheet that'll give you two 20 x 30-in. pieces at the home center for anywhere between $20 and $50.

T-Track parts: You'll need two each of these: 24-in. tracks, hold-down clamps, knobs and 2-1/2-in. T-Slot bolts. (These parts cost a total of about $50 available at rockler.com.)

PLANING WARPED BOARDS

A jointer is the best tool for flattening twisted, warped boards. But what if you don't have a jointer or the board is too wide? Set the board on a "sled," a flat piece of 3/4-in. plywood. Then shim the high corner(s) so the board doesn't rock. Also shim high spots in the middle of the board. Mark the shim locations, remove the board and hot-glue the shims into place. Then glue the board to the shims and the plywood with a dab of hot glue. Send that rascal through until it's flat, then pull it free and plane down the other side.

SLED BOARD

Tools & Skills: Shop Rat

ULTIMATE CLAMP RACK

If you have a big shop, a roll-around clamp rack is better than any wall-mounted system. It holds every type of clamp in one compact space, and you can wheel it right up to your work area. That saves miles of walking back and forth to the clamp rack.

This version is built from oak legs and 3/4-in. plywood shelves. Note that the front and back edges of the plywood are all the same length but have 7-degree bevels. The shorter pieces of edge trim also have 7-degree angles. When you cut the edge trim to length, it should be measured and cut to the bottom, longest part of each board.

Assemble the legs first and then preassemble the shelves. Then screw on the top and bottom shelves. Rest the rack upside down and slide in each shelf. Make sure they're evenly spaced and screw each one to the legs. Add the wheels, varnish it and you're done.

Figure A
Clamp rack

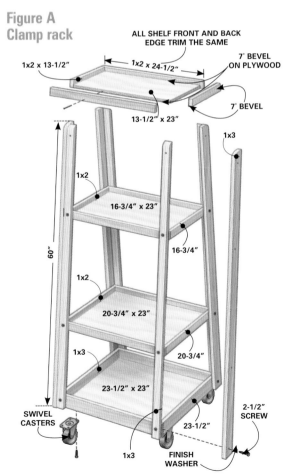

ALL SHELF FRONT AND BACK EDGE TRIM THE SAME

1x2 x 13-1/2"

1x2 x 24-1/2"

7° BEVEL ON PLYWOOD

7° BEVEL

13-1/2" x 23"

1x3

1x2

16-3/4" x 23"

16-3/4"

60"

1x2

20-3/4" x 23"

20-3/4"

1x3

23-1/2" x 23"

SWIVEL CASTERS

1x3

23-1/2"

FINISH WASHER

2-1/2" SCREW

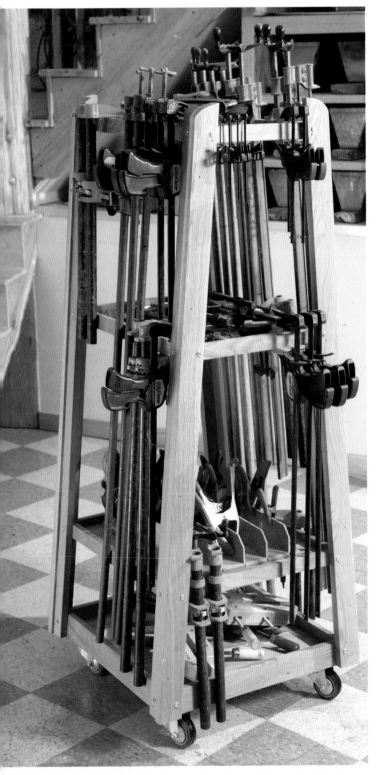

Yes, you can buy a clamp rack similar to this one for about $150, but why not have this good-looking version for a lot less? Plus it's another shop project!

MARKING AND CUTTING CURVES

Whether you're building a frame for an arched opening, making curved brackets or fashioning arch-top casing, marking and cutting curves is part of the process. Here we'll show you several techniques and tips for marking, cutting and fine-tuning curves. Some methods are best suited for rough curves. Others are refined enough for furniture making. Choose the technique that works best for the project at hand.

Cut precise curves with a router trammel

This simple router trammel is easy to build and allows you to cut a perfect circle. For circles up to 6 ft. across, use a piece of 1/4-in. plywood, MDF or hardboard that's about 4 ft. long and at least as wide as your router base. Start by removing the base plate from your router and clamping it to one end of the trammel material. If you want your trammel to be stylish, trace around a coffee cup to make a nice-looking rounded end. Then draw tangent lines connecting the circles and cut the sides. If you don't care about looks, simply make a long rectangular trammel.

Trace around the base plate and use the mounting holes as a guide for drilling holes in the trammel (**Photo 1**). Cut out the trammel and drill a 1-1/2-in. hole in the center of the router end to clear the router bit. Countersink the mounting screw holes so the screw heads won't tear up your workpiece. Attach the router to the trammel with the base plate screws.

Screw the trammel to the workpiece, centering it on the circle you want to cut out. Mount a straight plunge-cutting bit in your router and set the router bit to cut about 3/8 in. deep for the first pass. A plunge router works best, but if you don't have one, hold the router above the wood and start it. Carefully plunge it into the wood and begin moving it counterclockwise around the circle. Complete the circle, then readjust the depth and make another pass until you cut all the way through.

1 Lay out the trammel. **Draw the sides and ends of the trammel. Trace around the base plate and drill holes for the mounting screws.**

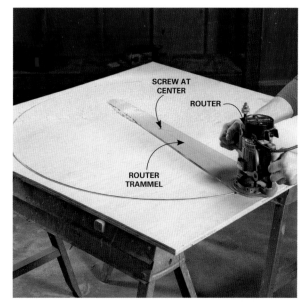

2 Rout a perfect circle. **Screw the trammel to the center of your workpiece and cut out the circle with your router. Make two or three passes in a counterclockwise direction.**

Tools & Skills

Cut gradual curves with a circular saw

The first tool that comes to mind for cutting curves is a jigsaw, but if the curve is gradual, try a circular saw instead. It's surprisingly quick and easy to cut a smooth curve with a circular saw. This method is for cutting rough curves. Don't try to make furniture with this technique. The trick is to make sure the curve is gradual enough that the blade doesn't bind. If you try this method and the blade binds or starts to heat up and smoke, switch to the jigsaw. The thinner the material you're cutting, the sharper the curve can be. Set the blade depth so it barely projects through the bottom of the wood.

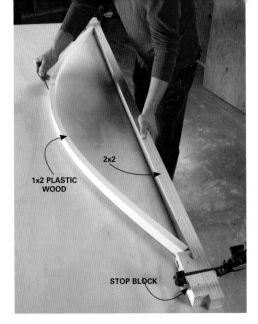

2x2

1x2 PLASTIC WOOD

STOP BLOCK

BLADE SET SHALLOW

Plastic wood template

Often you can simply "eyeball" the best curve for the job by bending a piece of wood and using it as a template. But variations in wood grain can result in inconsistent curves. Here's a tip to make this technique even better. Use plastic wood or a plastic molding instead. It bends very uniformly and yields near-perfect symmetrical curves. Azek, Fypon, Kleer and Versatex are several brands available at home centers. Choose a thickness that'll bend to the curve you need. For gradual bends or wide curves, use 3/4-in.-thick material. For tighter bends (those with a smaller radius), use a 1/2-in. x 1-1/4-in. plastic stop molding or something similar. Support the ends of the plastic wood with blocks attached to a strip of wood. Adjust the position of the blocks to change the curve.

Draw large curves with a giant compass

Grab any narrow board or strip of plywood and drill a few holes—voilà, instant compass. Drill a pencil-size hole a few inches from the end of the board. Then drill a screw-size hole at the pivot point. The distance between them should be the radius of the curve, if you know the measurement. Otherwise, just use the trial-and-error method, drilling a series of pivot holes until you can swing the trammel and draw the right-size arch. It's easy to draw parallel curves, too. Just drill two pencil holes spaced the desired distance apart.

There's no limit to the size of the arch you can draw. If your plan calls for a 10-ft. radius, find a long stick and use the floor as your workbench.

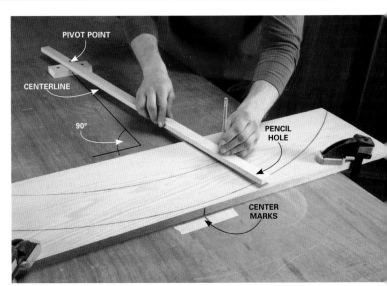

PIVOT POINT

CENTERLINE

90°

PENCIL HOLE

CENTER MARKS

Use a pattern and a router for irregular curves

When your plan calls for cutting curved parts and you need to make two or more, first shape and sand a perfect full-size pattern from a piece of 1/2-in. medium-density fiberboard. Then use a router with a top-bearing pattern bit to cut out the parts.

Here are a few tips for routing with a pattern bit. First use the pattern to mark the shape. Then remove excess material by cutting about 1/4 to 1/8 in. outside the lines with a jigsaw or a band saw. Elevate the workpiece to avoid cutting into your workbench. We used Bench Cookies (available at rockler.com; $12 for a set of four). But hot-melt glue and scraps of wood are another option. If you're cutting material that's thicker than the pattern bit is deep, cut as deep as you can. Then remove the pattern and use the part as the pattern to complete the cut.

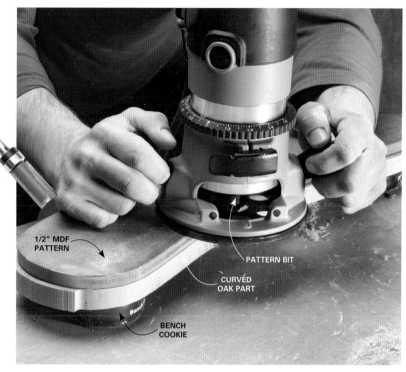

PATTERN BIT

1/2" MDF PATTERN

PATTERN BIT

CURVED OAK PART

BENCH COOKIE

Make matching parts with a pattern
Trace out and rough-cut your part. Attach the pattern with hot-melt glue. Use a top-bearing pattern bit to follow the pattern and shape the part. Move the router counterclockwise around the pattern.

Mark an arch with two sticks

Here's a quick way to draw an accurate curve if you know how wide and tall you want the arch to be. Let's say you want to draw an arch that's 3 ft. wide and 9 in. high. Drive two nails at the ends of the 3-ft. baseline. At the center of the baseline, draw a perpendicular line and make a mark 9 in. above the baseline. Drive a nail at the mark. At one end of the baseline, draw another perpendicular line and make another mark 9 in. above the baseline. Drive another nail at this mark. **Photo 1** shows how to arrange and connect two sticks that you will use to draw the arch (**Photo 2**).

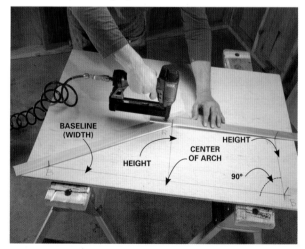

BASELINE (WIDTH)

HEIGHT

CENTER OF ARCH

HEIGHT

HEIGHT

90°

1 Set up for arch drawing with two sticks. **Drive nails at the ends of the baseline and at the height of the arch.** Lay one stick across two height nails and lay the other from the center height to the end of the baseline. Connect the sticks with short pins or hot-melt glue.

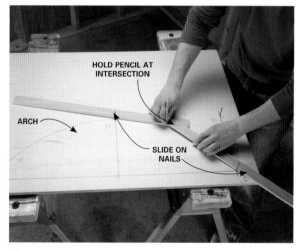

HOLD PENCIL AT INTERSECTION

ARCH

SLIDE ON NAILS

2 Slide the sticks over the nails. **Nestle a pencil into the crook of the sticks. With one end of the sticks resting on the baseline end nail and the other on the center height nail, slide the sticks along the nails to draw the arch. Repeat on the opposite side to complete the arch.**

SPECIAL SECTION
TOOLS & SKILLS

Tools & Skills
SUCCESS WITH MDF

Gary Wentz shares his experience

Medium-density fiber-board is the most versatile building material I know of. Because it's inexpensive and fairly durable, it's a good choice for practical projects like shelving and storage cabinets. But MDF is great for decorative projects, too. The smooth surface is perfect for painting, and a router leaves crisp profiles with no splintering, burning or tear-out.

Over the past 15 years, I've used MDF to build everything from crude shelving in my shop to fancy trim in upscale homes. I've even used it for furniture and ornate millwork like the trim board shown above. In fact, my own home is entirely trimmed out with MDF moldings made from about 50 sheets of MDF. Yes, I'm a fan of the stuff. This article will cover the most important things I've learned about working with MDF—and help you avoid some of the frustrating mistakes I've made.

MDF is basically sawdust and glue, fused together under pressure and heat. It varies in color from tan to chocolate brown. Common thicknesses range from 1/4 in. to 1 in., but most home centers carry only 1/2-in. and 3/4-in. Full sheets are oversized by 1 in., so a "4 x 8" sheet is actually 49 x 97 in. A full sheet of 3/4-in. MDF costs about $30. Some home centers also carry MDF boards in various lengths and widths. Working with MDF is no different from working with wood or plywood; you use the same tools to cut and shape it.

AVOID FULL SHEETS

I blame my hernia on MDF. A full sheet of 3/4-in. MDF weighs about 100 lbs., and I've lugged lots of them from my pickup to my shop. But there are ways to avoid hernia surgery:

- Buy half (4 x 4-ft.) or quarter (2 x 4-ft.) sheets instead of full sheets.
- Some lumberyards and home centers sell MDF shelving, usually in 1 x 8-ft. sections ($6). I like to slice these long, easy-to-handle shelves into trim stock.
- Some home centers and lumberyards will cut full sheets into manageable sections at no extra charge.

PREPARE FOR A DUST STORM

There's one thing you'll really hate about MDF: the fine, powdery dust that invades your clothes, hangs in the air for hours and clings to every surface like a coat of frost. Cutting MDF is a dusty job, but routing it is even worse.

Whenever possible, I cut and rout MDF outside. When that's not possible, I drape sheets of plastic over shelving and other hard-to-clean areas in my shop and use a fan to blow dust outside. When installing trim in a room, cover doorways, close air vents and expect to vacuum every surface when you're done, even the walls. Clean your vacuum filter often—the fine dust plugs filters quickly. And a tight-fitting dust mask is essential.

FAN IN WINDOW

MAKE YOUR OWN TRIM—CHEAP!

When a job calls for painted trim, I almost always cut costs with MDF. Even inexpensive wood, like this poplar baseboard, costs four times as much. To make trim, I cut MDF sheets into strips and shape the edges with a router or router table. With the right bit, I can create just about any trim profile, simple or fancy. Eagleamerica.com is one good place to browse for bits. Bits that cut baseboard profiles like the one shown here cost from $40 to $70. Some home centers carry ready-made MDF trim; baseboard similar to the trim shown here costs about $1.70 per foot.

PAINT-GRADE WOOD BASEBOARD: $2.65 PER FT.

HOMEMADE MDF BASEBOARD: 62¢ PER FT.

DON'T DROP IT

The face of MDF is harder than most woods, but the inner layers are soft. So edges, and especially corners, are easy to crush. That means you have to handle it with more care than lumber or plywood. Also avoid scratching the face. Light scratches stand out like a sore thumb on the ultra-smooth surface, so you have to sand them out completely before priming. And wear gloves when handling MDF, especially when carrying heavy sheets. MDF edges can be sharp enough to cut skin—I've got the scars to prove it.

COMBINE MDF WITH WOOD MOLDINGS

Here's one of my favorite tricks for painted trim, cabinets or even furniture: Use MDF for the large, plain parts and dress them up with wood moldings like base cap, coves or base shoe. That gives you the money savings of MDF without the time-consuming work of making MDF trim from scratch. The wainscoting shown here, for example, is simply panels and strips of 1/2-in. MDF trimmed with small-profile pine moldings that cost less than 75¢ per foot. The cap rail is likely to take a beating from chairs, so I make that from wood instead of MDF. Once coated with primer and paint, the wood and MDF parts will look exactly the same.

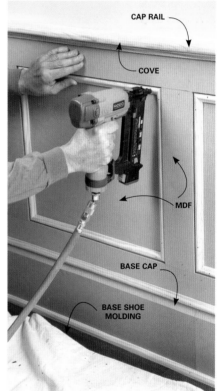

CAP RAIL

COVE

MDF

BASE CAP

BASE SHOE MOLDING

DON'T DRIVE WITHOUT DRILLING

MDF is kind of like an Oreo cookie: two hard faces with a softer core between them. That soft core splits easily when you drive a screw into the edge. The hard face presents different problems for screws. If you don't drill a countersink recess, the screw head may snap off before it sinks into the MDF. Or, if the head does sink, it might push up chips. The cure for both problems is to use a countersinking drill bit ($4), which gives you a pilot hole and a recess for the screw head in one step.

COUNTERSINK BIT

Tools & Skills

SAND, PRIME, SAND...

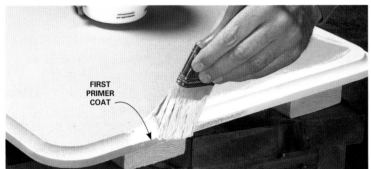

FIRST PRIMER COAT

The face of MDF is smooth, but the edges are fuzzy like the skin of a peach. If you just slap paint on the fuzz, it will look and feel like sandpaper. So you have to get rid of the peach fuzz before you paint. I have two recipes for smooth edges: one for "good-enough" edges and the other for edges that will get a high-gloss finish.

Here's the good-enough process I apply to most projects, including trim: First, lightly sand the edges with 100-grit paper. Foam-backed sanding pads work great on routed profiles. Then prime the MDF. Use a solvent-based primer only. Water-based primer can raise small blisters. My favorite MDF primers are KILZ and Cover Stain because they're easy to sand. When the primer dries, sand off the fuzz with 100-grit pads. A couple of light passes is all it takes. You can sand KILZ or

SANDING PAD

Cover Stain after a couple of hours, but let the primer dry overnight for smoother results. After sanding, wipe away the powdery dust with a damp cloth and you're ready to paint.

For projects that will get a coat of high-gloss paint, I prime twice: First I prime the edges only. Later I prime the whole project (as described above). When applying the edge-only coat, be sure to feather out any primer on the face of the MDF so brush marks won't show up later. Then sand, prime again and sand again to achieve smooth-as-glass edges.

DON'T LET IT GET WET

MDF stands up to moisture about as well as graham crackers. A few water drops will raise small bumps on the surface. A long soaking will make it swell to twice its original thickness. So MDF is a risky choice for baseboards in entryways and trim near tubs or sinks. My all-time greatest MDF mistake was using it for windowsills in my own home. Condensation from the windows made them swell just like the baseboard shown here. If you use MDF as baseboard, be sure to paint the lower edge before installation. That will provide short-term protection against occasional spills. Also install the baseboard about 1/4 in. above the floor and then cover the gap with wood base shoe molding. There are moisture-resistant versions of MDF, but they're hard to find. To find manufacturers and dealers, search online for "moisture resistant MDF."

DON'T USE A HAMMER

Unless you're willing to drill a hole for every single nail, don't plan on using a hammer. Without a hole, the nail will probably bend in rock-hard MDF. And even if it goes in without bending, the nail will push up a mound of fiber that looks like a mini volcano. A trim nailer, on the other hand, shoots nails through MDF every time. The skinny nails will raise tiny pimples, but you can easily scrape them off with a sharp putty knife before you fill the nail holes.

Question&Answer

WHEN TO USE A ROTARY DRILL

I'm installing a sprinkler system and have to drill a 1-in. hole through my poured concrete foundation for the water line. I own a hammer drill with a 1/2-in. chuck and was able to find a 1-in. masonry bit with a 1/2-in. shank, but it was too short. Can I just mount it in an extension?

Probably not. Those extensions aren't designed to take abuse from a hammer drill. Even if you didn't need an extension, the 1-in. bit likely exceeds the rated capacity of your hammer drill. As a rule, a heavy-duty 1/2-in. hammer drill is limited to a 3/4-in. bit. Even if you could find a stepped-down shank that you could chuck into your drill, you're better off renting a rotary hammer drill with the proper length bit. It'll get the job done in a fraction of the time and with a lot less sweat.

1/2" HAMMER DRILL

3/4" ROTARY DRILL

HOLE SAW HASSLES

I dread using hole saws in wood or metal. Wood takes forever, and metal dulls the teeth. I'm also confused by the different varieties—and the huge price range. Which type should I get? Is there a way to speed up the drilling process?

We talked to Matt Savarino, the hole saw expert at Lenox Tools, to get to the bottom of your dilemma. Matt told us that most DIYers don't need expensive hole saws. In fact, for occasional cuts in wood, he says the cheapest carbon steel saws work just fine (see **Photo 1**). But don't try using them in metal—that'll destroy the saw teeth in seconds.

But if you're cutting a hole in your steel door for a dead bolt, or cut lots of holes, step up to a bimetal hole saw. The teeth are made from a harder steel than the shell, so they last longer. But that doesn't mean they're indestructible. Always provide lubrication when drilling into metal. Cutting oil is best, and even ordinary motor oil is better than nothing (see **Photo 2**). You can use bimetal saws to cut through all types of materials except ceramic, porcelain, granite and the like. For those, you need a carbide-grit hole saw.

Even if you drill relief holes, hole saws take forever to drill through thick wood. If the holes are less than 1-1/2 in. in diameter, don't bother with hole saws; use spade bits.

1 Holes in wood. **The best way to cut holes faster is to drill relief holes to exhaust wood chips and keep the blade cooler.**

2 Holes in metal. **In metal, always use bimetal hole saws and keep the teeth sharper longer by using lubricating oil.**

Tools & Skills: Question & Answer

AIR COMPRESSOR QUANDARY

My old air compressor pooped out and I need a new one. I see air compressors advertised for less than $100. Are they even worth having?

It all depends on how much you'll be running it, and what you plan to use it for. Compressors that cost less than $100 are very portable and will do a fine job of running a trim nailer, filling tires or blowing dust off your clothes—but that's about it. You'll have to be patient; they take a long time to get up to pressure and to fill tires. If you do decide on a cheap compressor, consider it a "throw-away" tool and be prepared to replace it when it dies. Virtually any repair will exceed the replacement cost.

If you can afford to spend about $300, you can get a portable compressor that'll power most DIY air tools and last for a couple of decades (see **Photo 2**). Look for a compressor with a cast iron cylinder, oil lubrication and air output of at least 4 cu. ft. per minute (cfm). You'll have to change the oil on schedule to keep it humming. But the longer life outweighs the hassle. Also be aware that

oil-lubricated compressors inject a fine oil mist into the air line. So you'll need to invest in a separate hose and a filter if you're going to use a paint sprayer.

You can find less expensive, oilless compressors ($129 to $199) that will put out 4 cfm, but don't expect them to last as long. And you'll need to wear hearing protection—they're LOUD!

If you're a serious motorhead, you'll have to take a larger leap. If you want to run "air-motor" powered tools like impact wrenches and ratchets, you'll have to get serious with a unit that's capable of at least 5.5 cfm with a sizable air tank. Just forget about running air-powered sanders and sandblasters—those guys require almost 9 cfm (see **Photo 3**). Expect to spend $540 plus for a good one. But the only thing that makes them portable is the wheels. They're heavy and bulky.

$89 • .7 CFM • OILLESS

1 Run your brad nailers all day with a low-cost air compressor. It'll run a framing nailer, too, but you'll have to wait for the pressure to rebuild after every few nails.

MAKITA

$300 • 4.2 CFM • OIL SPLASH LUBRICATION

2 Pony up more money to get a quality portable oil-lube compressor that's powerful enough to run all these air tools, including a framing nailer.

CAMPBELL HAUSFELD

$540 • 5.8 CFM • OIL LUBRICATION

3 Blast big bolts with a powerful impact wrench and a heavy-duty compressor. This model has a 20-gallon tank, twin pistons and a fully cast iron pump.

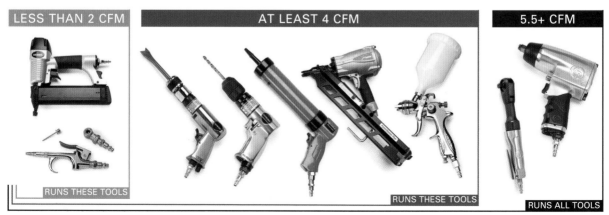

LESS THAN 2 CFM

AT LEAST 4 CFM

5.5+ CFM

RUNS THESE TOOLS

RUNS THESE TOOLS

RUNS ALL TOOLS

GRAB 'N GO
TOOL STORAGE

Do you spend too much time looking for tools on shelves scattered around your garage? If so, this grab-and-go tool cabinet is the answer. You corral all your power tools and accessories in one place and roll them around your garage or shop. The pullout table is great for doing quick repairs, prepping tools and sorting parts. The drawers are removable totes that you can carry to your work area.

You'll also like how easy it is to build. All the parts are glued and screwed together with simple butt joints and overlays. Just build the top section of tool bins first, then build the lower shelving unit to slide under.

Time, money & materials

You can easily build the cabinet in one weekend and then apply the finish and install the hardware the next. Figure on spending about $375 for the entire project including hardware and finish. We chose 3/4-in. birch plywood for the main structure and 1/2-in. plywood for the backs and drawer sides. You'll also need hardwood for the drawer fronts and the edges of the pullout work surface. You can

dress up the look with simple moldings to cover the exposed plywood faces.

Build the upper bins first

Cut the plywood parts according to the Cutting List on p. 46. Assemble each of the three bins as shown in **Photo 1**. To make assembly faster, we used self-drilling screws, which means you won't need a pilot hole or a countersink. However, drill a shallow starter hole with a 3/32-in. bit to keep the tip of the screw from wandering off the mark as you start to drive the screw.

When you join the three bins (**Photo 2**), you'll need a work surface that's absolutely flat; an old flush panel door

Meet a pro: David Radtke
David is a custom cabinetmaker, home design consultant, freelance editor and home restoration specialist in Minneapolis. He enjoys archery, bowmaking, woodturning and cycling—whenever he's not standing behind a table saw or sitting in front of the drawing board.

Figure A Tool cabinet

Overall dimensions:
60-1/2" tall x 61-1/4" wide
x 17" deep

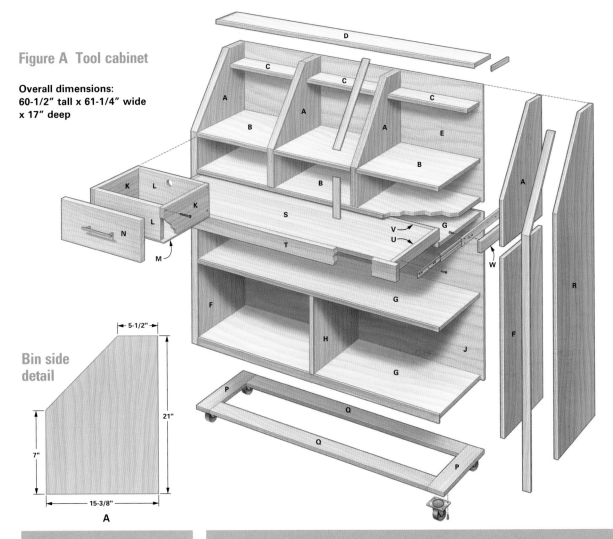

Bin side detail

5-1/2"

21"

7"

15-3/8"

A

MATERIALS LIST

ITEM	QTY.
3/4" hardwood plywood	4
1/2" hardwood plywood	2
1/4" x 3/4" screen molding	40'
1/4" x 1-1/2" lattice	20'
3/4" x 1-1/2" (hardwood table edging)	5'
1x8 hardwood (drawer facing)	5'
1x4 hardwood (table front)	5'
14" ball-bearing drawer slides	2
3" swivel casters	4
5" drawer pulls	3
8"-wide drawer pulls	2
Wood glue	1 pint
No. 8 x 1-1/4" screws	1 box
No. 8 x 1-1/2" screws	1 box
5/16" x 1-1/2" lag screws	16
1-1/4" 18-gauge nails	1 box
7/8" pneumatic staples	1 box

CUTTING LIST

KEY	QTY.	SIZE & DESCRIPTION
A	6	3/4" x 15-3/8" x 21" bin sides
B	6	3/4" x 15-3/8" x 18" bin shelves
C	3	3/4" x 5" x 18" upper bin shelves
D	1	3/4" x 7" x 60-3/4" top
E*	1	1/2" x 21" x 58-1/4" upper assembly back
F	2	3/4" x 15-3/8" x 32" lower unit sides
G*	3	3/4" x 15-3/8" x 56-7/8" lower unit shelves
H	1	3/4" x 15-3/8" x 14-13/16" lower unit vertical partition
J*	1	1/2" x 32" x 58-1/4" lower unit back
K	6	1/2" x 15-3/8" x 5-1/4" drawer sides
L*	6	3/4" x 17" x 5-1/4" drawer fronts and backs
M*	3	1/4" x 15-3/8" x 17-7/8" plywood drawer bottoms

KEY	QTY.	SIZE & DESCRIPTION
N	3	3/4" x 6-5/8" x 19-1/4" hardwood drawer face
P	2	3/4" x 3-1/2" x 15-3/4" plywood side base supports
Q*	2	3/4" x 3-1/2" x 51-3/16" plywood front and back base supports
R	2	3/4" x 15-7/8" x 55-7/8" plywood finished sides
S*	1	3/4" x 14-5/8" x 54-3/8" plywood pullout table
T*	1	3/4" x 3-1/4" x 58-1/4" hardwood table face
U*	2	3/4" x 1-1/2" x 15-3/8" hardwood table side edging
V*	1	3/4" x 1-1/2" x 54-3/8" hardwood table back edging
W	2	3/4" x 2" x 15-3/8" plywood spacers

* Measure and cut to fit

on sawhorses works perfectly for this. Finish the bin unit by gluing and nailing the top into place (**Photo 3**).

Making the drawers fit

Measure the openings in the bottom of the bins and then downsize the drawer about 1/8 in. in total height and width. Since the drawers don't have slides, this will give you just the right clearance. Take into account the thickness of the plywood drawer bottom. Sometimes "1/4-in. plywood" is actually 3/16 in. thick.

Build the lower shelving section

Measure the width of the top assembly and then cut the parts for the lower shelving unit so it'll be exactly the same width. "Three-quarter-inch" plywood isn't exactly 3/4 in. thick; it's actually 23/32 in. That's why it's critical to measure. Use the Cutting List as a guide, but measure carefully to be sure.

Screw the sides to the shelves using Figure A as your guide. Install the lower partition (H) halfway between the bottom and middle shelf. Cut the 1/2-in. plywood back and check the assembly for square, then glue and nail it to the back of the sides and shelf.

To reinforce the bottom shelf, rip 3-1/2-in. strips of 3/4-in. plywood (parts P and Q) and glue and nail them to the bottom of the assembly. Screw the casters to the strips.

Combine the two sections

Mount the drawer slide that will support the pullout table (**Photo 5**). Then lay the upper unit onto its back and glue and screw the outer sides (R) to the bin sides (A). You may need to shim underneath to bring the sides perfectly flush.

Next slide the lower unit into the upper until it contacts the spacers (W). Align the faces of the lower assembly with the outer sides (R) and drive the screws from the inside. You'll need nine screws per side.

At this stage, the project has acquired considerable heft, so get someone to help you tip it upright.

1 Build the bins. **Position the shelves with spacers and tack them in place with a brad nailer. Then add screws for strength.**

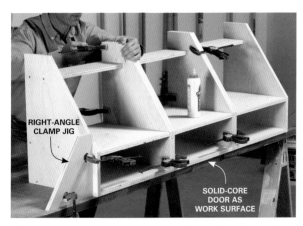

2 Join the bins. **Line them up on a flat surface, then glue and clamp them together. A homemade squaring jig holds the bins square until the back is on.**

3 Add the back and top. **First glue and nail on the back. Then sand the front edges of the bins so they're flush. Finally, glue and nail on the top.**

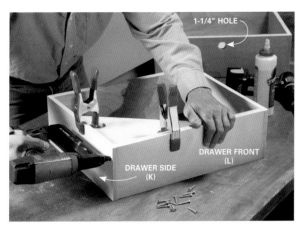

4 Build the drawers. **Tack them together with nails and glue, then add screws. A squaring jig makes square assembly easy. Drill holes through the back of each drawer to act as a handle.**

Nail on the edging

Now you can cut and glue the edge banding to the exposed plywood edges. We used screen molding for the 3/4-in. faces and 1/4-in.-thick lattice for the double-thick faces. You may need to rip the lattice to fit. Keep in mind that you don't want the trim to hang over and obstruct the drawer openings, so be sure to flush the edging with the plywood.

Finishing touches

With the unit nearly finished, you can now make the pullout table. Carefully measure the distance between the side spacers. Subtract 1 in. from this measurement (1/2-in. clearance for each drawer slide) and build the table to this precise width. Now you can cut and screw the drawer faces to the front of the drawers. Be sure you have 1/4-in. clearance between the bottom of the drawer faces and the pullout table. Align the edges of the outer drawer faces so they're even with the table front.

For a fast, easy finish, use a wipe-on polyurethane or Watco oil. Use a brush to get into tight areas and then a lint-free rag to wipe the finish. Let dry and give it a second coat.

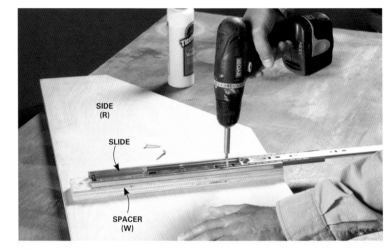

5 Mount the slides for the pullout table. **Glue and nail spacers to sides, then add the slides. This is a lot easier to do before you attach the sides to the bins.**

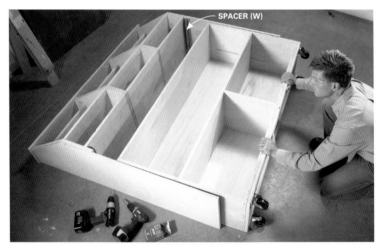

6 Combine the upper and lower units. **Slide the lower unit into the upper unit until it makes contact with the spacers. Screw the lower unit to the sides.**

7 Cover exposed plywood edges. **If the trim is a bit too wide, you can shave it slightly with your table saw. Glue and nail the edging into place.**

4 Exterior Maintenance & Repairs

IN THIS CHAPTER

HOW TO REPAIR **MORTAR JOINTS**

Crumbling masonry joints start out ugly, and then things get uglier fast—bricks come loose, water seeps behind the wall and bees make their homes in the mortar holes. Let it go and the problem won't go away. In fact, the deterioration will accelerate and you'll have a much bigger fix on your hands. But you can mend the joints yourself with a process called tuckpointing.

Tuckpointing isn't difficult or expensive—the only real investment is your time. But you can pick away at it in your free time, area by area.

The steps we show here will work on any brick walls, chimneys and retaining walls. Tuckpointing won't fix cracking or crumbling bricks, or cracks in walls caused by a shifting foundation. Those problems call for more drastic fixes that we won't cover here.

Pick up tools and materials

First and foremost, you'll need an angle grinder with a 4- or 4-1/4-in. diamond blade. Don't bother renting one unless you only have several feet of bad joints. You can buy one for as little as $40—even a fairly cheap one will do the trick (unless you're a serious tool junkie or you have an entire house that needs extensive tuckpointing).

You'll also need a few simple, inexpensive specialty tools that are available at masonry suppliers and some home centers. You'll need a brick trowel ($10) and a tuck pointer ($11). If you have concave mortar joints, you'll need a masonry jointer ($4) that's the width of your joints. For flat joints, you'll need a joint raker ($9). If you have just a few areas that need work, use a hammer and cold chisel

to knock out the old mortar, but for more extensive work, plan on getting a rotary hammer drill fitted with a flat chisel to make the job go a heck of a lot quicker. You can rent one for $40 per day. If you have days' worth of work, rental costs can break the bank. In that case, spend the $120 (or more) to own one.

You'll also need mortar mix. A 60-lb. bag costs $4 at home centers. If you need colored mortar, take a small piece of the old mortar to a masonry supplier and ask for help finding a mortar dye to match. But be aware of this— fresh tuckpointing always stands out against older mortar. However, it will eventually weather to match.

Start small

If you only have a few joints to tuckpoint, dive right in. But if you have a large wall to tackle, start in a small area to get a feel for the operation before you start hogging out entire walls. You'll hone your skills and get a good idea of how much you can tuckpoint at one time. You'll have 30 to 60 minutes of working time once you mix the mortar.

Get ready for the dust

Tuckpointing is a dirty business. Grinding the joints creates a dust storm, with chunks of mortar covering the

1 **Grind the horizontal joints first. Grind along the top and bottom of the horizontal joints. Get as close to the bricks as you can. If you accidentally grind against the bricks, the dust will turn the color of the brick.**

2 **Plunge-cut the vertical joints. Grind both sides of the vertical joints. Plunge the grinder into the joint and work it up and down to make the cuts. But be careful not to grind the bricks above and below the joints.**

ground. Spread a drop cloth on the ground to catch the mortar so cleanup will take minutes instead of hours.

Close your house windows to keep out the dust, and tell your neighbors who might be affected to do the same.

Grind out the joints

Before you can put new mortar in the joints, you have to cut out the damaged material. Start by grinding the top and bottom of the horizontal (bed) joints with an angle grinder (Photo 1). Hold the grinder with both hands to keep it steady and avoid grinding into the bricks. You only need to grind 3/4 in. into the mortar.

Start at outside corners and work inward. That keeps you from putting extra pressure on the corner bricks, which could knock them out of the wall. After you've finished the horizontal joints, do the vertical (head) joints (Photo 2).

Knock out the mortar

Use the rotary hammer drill to pound the mortar out of the joints. Set the drill on the rotating mode (it puts less pressure on the bricks). Again, work from the outside corners inward (Photo 3). Keep the chisel point in the mortar joint and keep moving the hammer. The drill makes quick work of removing mortar, but be careful. The powerful tool can also knock out bricks. If that happens, take them all the way out, chisel off all the mortar, then reset them when you fill the joints.

There's really no secret to knocking out the mortar. Just hold the drill at about a 45-degree angle to the wall, squeeze the trigger and watch the mortar fall out. **Caution: Wear eye protection—mortar pieces can go flying!**

Clean out the joints

Once you've chipped out the damaged mortar, use a hand broom to sweep the joints. Sweep away mortar clumps and the dust (Photo 4). Use the rotary hammer drill to bust out stubborn chunks.

Then wash out the joints with water. But don't hose down the wall or you'll soak everything, including the ground where you'll be standing or kneeling. Instead, fill a bucket with water and brush the water into the joints (Photo 5). Don't worry about slopping water onto the bricks—you want them damp before you fill the joints anyway.

Mix the new mortar

If you're tinting the mortar, stir the dye and the mortar mix in a bucket before adding the water. Dye is typically sold in 1-1/2-lb. bags. Mix one-quarter of the dye with one-quarter of a 60-lb. bag of mortar mix. Stir in water until the mix is the consistency of peanut butter (Photo 6).

3 Hammer out the mortar. Keep moving the rotary hammer drill along the joints as you chisel out the mortar. Be sure to keep the chisel off the bricks so you don't knock them out of place.

4 Sweep out the joints. Use a small broom to sweep debris and dust out of the joints. Inspect the joints for any remaining stubborn mortar and knock it out with the drill.

5 Give the joints a bath. Stick a brush into a bucket of water and rinse out the joints. Your goal here isn't to make surfaces pristine, just to get rid of chunks and dust.

6 Whip up the mortar batch. Mix the mortar to the consistency of peanut butter with no dry spots or clumps. You'll know the mix is right when it sticks to your trowel when you hold it at a 45-degree angle. Let the mortar sit for 10 minutes before using it.

7 Fill the joints. **Load your brick trowel and hold it next to the joint. Work the mortar into the joint with your tuck pointer. Pack the joint full before moving on to the next one.**

8 Strike the mortar joints. **Drag the jointer along the vertical joints and the horizontal joints. Apply gentle pressure to tool out the ridges where the joints intersect. Finish one joint before moving on to the next.**

9 Wipe down the bricks. **Scrub the mortar off the bricks with a stiff brush. This also knocks down and smooths out any high spots along the joint edges.**

The mortar will last 30 to 60 minutes, but you may need to add water to keep it workable. After one hour, throw out what's left and mix a new batch.

Work the mortar into the joints

Use a brick trowel and a tuck pointer to pack the mortar into the joints. Most pros prefer this method to using a grout/mortar bag. Mortar that is hand packed is more durable.

Scoop mortar onto the trowel. Hold the trowel next to the joint, then press the mortar into the joint with the tuck pointer (**Photo 7**). Pack the joint until it's flush with the front of the bricks.

Tool the joints

Let the mortar in the filled joints set for about 30 minutes. If you're tuckpointing a large area, continually check the first joints you filled to see if they're ready to tool (finish). Check by pressing the filled joint with your thumb. If your thumb leaves only a slight impression, it's ready to tool. If it goes in deeper, wait five minutes and try again. But don't let the mortar get too stiff—it can start to harden after just 30 minutes, making it difficult to tool the joints.

If you want rounded joints, press a masonry jointer into the top of vertical joints and pull the tool downward. The jointer will push out some of the mortar and leave a concave shape. For horizontal joints, start at a corner (**Photo 8**). Run the tool about halfway across the joint, then stop and finish tooling from the other side.

For flat joints, place a joint raker over an old joint to set the depth. Then run the raker along the new joints to make them flat.

Clean the bricks

Once the joints have set up (about 30 minutes after tooling), use a stiff-bristle brush to clean dried mortar off the bricks (**Photo 9**).

If the mortar refuses to come off, wait three days, then use muriatic acid ($7 for 1 gallon at home centers). Use 10 parts water to 1 part acid (add the acid to the water, not the other way around). **Caution: Be sure to wear eye protection and rubber gloves when working with acid.** Brush the acid onto the bricks with a stiff-bristle brush, scrub the bricks and let the acid fizz. Then rinse the acid off with water. If there's still a little mortar residue left, treat it again.

The acid can slightly alter the bricks' appearance, so test it on a small area first. If it does alter the appearance, increase the ratio of water to acid.

PATCH **ROTTED WOOD**

Do you have rotted wood? It's usually better to simply tear out the old board or molding and replace it than to repair it. But for windowsills and door jambs that are hard to remove and molding that would be tough to duplicate, patching with wood filler makes sense.

Fillers for repair of rotted wood generally fall into three categories. For small holes and cracks, there are fillers like DAP Latex Wood Filler or MH Ready Patch that harden as the water or solvent evaporates. Other fillers, such as Durham's Rock Hard Water Putty, harden by a chemical reaction when water is mixed in. Finally, two-part fillers like Minwax High Performance Wood Filler (polyester) and Abatron's WoodEpox (epoxy) harden after you mix the two parts.

Two-part fillers are the most durable, and the best choice for long-lasting repairs. Although polyester and epoxy are both two-part fillers, they have unique characteristics that make them quite different to work with. We'll show you the differences and give you some tips for working with these two excellent wood repair fillers.

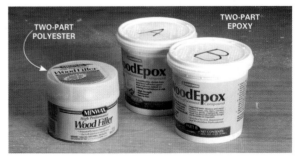

Epoxy and polyester fillers are two-part formulas that harden after you mix the parts. They're both excellent fillers, though with slightly different characteristics.

ROTTED WOOD

1 Gouge out rotted wood with a chisel, screwdriver or other pointy tool.

Use epoxy for a premium repair

One common brand of epoxy wood filler is Abatron WoodEpox (abatron.com; 800-445-1754). A kit containing pints of LiquidEpoxy consolidant parts A and B and WoodEpox parts A and B costs $76. Unlike polyester filler, epoxy wood filler has a dough-like consistency, so it will stay put even on vertical repairs.

Prepare for an epoxy repair by removing as much rotted wood as possible. Use an old screwdriver, chisel or 5-in-1 painter's tool to gouge out the damaged wood (**Photo 1**). If the wood is wet, cover it loosely with a poly tent and let it dry completely before starting the repair. Drill a series of 1/4-in. holes around the rotted area if you suspect rotted wood below the surface, but don't drill all the way through. You'll fill these with consolidant to solidify the wood around the repair.

Start the repair by soaking the damaged area with epoxy consolidant (**Photo 2**). Mix the consolidant according to the directions. Wear rubber gloves and safety glasses when you're working with epoxy. You can mix the consolidant in a squirt bottle or a small plastic container. Use a disposable brush to work the epoxy consolidant into the wood fibers. Epoxy is difficult to remove after it hardens, so clean up drips and runs right away with paper towels. You don't have to wait

Tips for working with epoxy:

- Label the caps "A" and "B" and don't mix them up.
- Start with a clean container or mixing board each time you mix a new batch.
- Save epoxy by filling most of the cavity with a scrap of wood. Glue it in with epoxy filler.
- Carve the epoxy before it becomes rock hard.

8-OZ. GRADUATED SQUEEZE BOTTLE

NITRILE RUBBER GLOVES

2 Mix two-part epoxy consolidant in a squeeze bottle. Squirt it into the holes and repair area. Use a disposable brush to spread the consolidant and work it into the wood fibers.

MIXING BOARD

3 Mix the two-part epoxy wood filler on a smooth board according to the manufacturer's directions.

SOFT EPOXY WOOD FILLER

4 Press the epoxy filler into the repair. Leave enough protruding so you can shape the repair after it starts to harden.

for the consolidant to harden before applying the epoxy filler.

Next mix the two-part epoxy filler on a mixing board (**Photo 3**). Then apply it with a putty knife or simply press it into place with your fingers (**Photo 4**). Roughly shape the epoxy, making sure it protrudes beyond the final profile. When the temperature is 70° F, you'll have about 30 minutes before the epoxy starts to harden. Increase the working time by spreading the epoxy in a thin layer on your mixing board and keeping it cool. On a warm day, the epoxy will harden enough in three or four hours to start shaping it with a Surform plane, rasp and sandpaper (**Photo 5**). After rough-shaping with a plane or rasp, sand the filler with 80-grit and then 120-grit sandpaper. If you sand off too much (or didn't add enough epoxy to begin with), dust off the repair and add another layer. You can make a more spreadable filler by mixing a small batch of consolidant and a small batch of filler and then adding some of the consolidant to the filler to reach the desired consistency.

HARDENED EPOXY WOOD FILLER

5 Rough out the shape with a rasp. Mix another batch of epoxy filler and add another layer, if necessary. Fine-tune the repair with sandpaper, then prime and paint.

Polyester is readily available and less expensive

If you've done any auto body repair, you've probably worked with two-part polyester filler. Minwax High Performance Wood Filler is one brand formulated for wood repair, but a gallon container of Bondo or some other brand of two-part auto body polyester will also work and may be less expensive for larger fixes.

The process for repairing wood is much the same whether you're using polyester filler or epoxy. Instead of epoxy consolidant, you'll use High Performance Wood Hardener to solidify and strengthen the wood fibers (**Photo 1**). Polyester begins hardening faster than Abatron WoodEpox. Depending on the temperature, you'll have about 10 to 15 minutes to work before the filler starts to harden.

Also, unlike WoodEpox, polyester tends to sag when you're doing vertical repairs. One trick is to build a form and line it with plastic sheeting. Press the form against the filler and attach it with screws. Then pull it off after the filler hardens. Or you can wait until the sagging filler reaches the hardness of soap and carve it off with a putty knife or chisel or shape it with a Surform plane or rasp (**Photo 2**). Most medium to large repairs will require at least two layers of filler. Complete the repair by sanding and priming the filled area and then painting.

1 Remove rotted wood with a 5-in-1 or other sharp tool. Then coat the area with wood hardener as shown. Mix polyester wood filler and press it into the recess with a putty knife.

2 Carve the partially hardened sagging wood filler with a putty knife or chisel. Add another layer of filler, if necessary.

INSTALL A
NEW ENTRY DOOR

A new door in one day? Let pro Jeff Gorton teach you a few new tricks!

Robin and Danny's front door was dented and drafty. They needed a new door, and we needed a place to photograph a door installation story. It was a perfect match. Robin and Danny agreed to install the door themselves with my help. I've installed dozens of doors throughout my carpentry career, so I knew how to guide them through the pitfalls. I have to confess, though, there were a few times when I couldn't resist jumping in to lend a hand. Still, the new homeowners did a great job of tearing out the old door and installing a new one. The new door looked terrific—we were all happy with the results. Here's how we went about the project.

One of the biggest mistakes homeowners make is to grab a door off the home center shelf and expect it to fit right. So my first coaching task was to help Robin and Danny measure for and order the door. First we measured the width and height of the door. Then Robin carefully pried off the interior trim (**Photo 1**) so we could measure the rough opening, which is the width between the studs and the height from the floor to the header. Next we measured from the back of the outside trim, or brick molding, to the face of the interior wall to find the jamb width. Ordering the new door with the right jamb width ensures that the interior trim fits without the need for added jamb extensions. Finally we went back outside and measured the width from the outside of the brick molding and the height from the bottom of the sill to the top of the exterior trim. To avoid having to patch siding, it's best to order a door assembly that will fill the space. This may mean asking for special exterior trim that's wider than standard 2-in.-wide "brick molding." If you're ordering a door and sidelight(s), you can adjust the width by substituting a different size sidelight or by adjusting the space between the door and the sidelight. The door and sidelight were assembled at the plant and arrived as a single unit. Installation of a door without a sidelight is the same.

With the door size, jamb width and dimensions of the rough and exterior opening in hand, Robin and Danny went door shopping. They discovered that the standard configuration of a 3-ft. door and sidelight was a few inches too narrow and 1/2 in. shorter than their existing door and sidelight. The salesperson recommended spending a little extra

> **"Protecting the wall with a putty knife saved the wall paint. Neat trick!"**
> — **Robin**

1 Pry off the interior trim. Robin thought this was a pretty neat trick. Protecting the wall with a putty knife under the pry bar meant she wouldn't have to repaint the entry.

BRICK MOLDING

2 Tear off the brick molding. Danny cut the caulk along the edges of the brick molding with a utility knife so it would be easier to remove. But the molding was still stubborn and came off in pieces.

money to add a spacer between the door and the sidelight. This corrected the width problem. Robin and Danny could have ordered a custom height door and frame for several hundred dollars more, but they decided to live with the height difference and cover the gap with trim later. We decided to add a strip of plywood under the sill to raise the door slightly, so in the end the shorter height worked out perfectly.

Robin and Danny wanted a door that looked like wood, minus the maintenance hassles. They chose a Therma-Tru fiberglass door with a surprisingly realistic-looking oak wood grain. The cost of the door and sidelight unit was $1,300. Fortunately (for us, anyway!), the door assembly plant wasn't too busy and the door was delivered about 10 days later.

Remove the old door

Robin was surprised at how easy the door and frame were to remove, especially after the interior and exterior trim were off (Photos 1 and 2). And she got to learn a new skill—operating a reciprocating saw (Photo 3). If you don't have a recip saw, you can use a hacksaw blade. Working in older houses or where the door is exposed to the weather, I often have to repair a water-damaged subfloor or otherwise rebuild the sill area before installing the new door. In this case, the subfloor was in good condition, but we noticed that the new door sill was thinner than the old one. After taking a few measurements, we decided to add a strip of plywood over the subfloor to raise the door so it would clear the entry rug (Photo 5). Robin checked to be sure the sill area was level. We could have shimmed under the plywood with strips of building paper or scrap vinyl flooring to level the floor, if necessary.

Since our door was covered by an overhanging roof, we didn't need additional

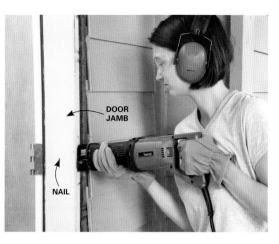

3 Free the door frame. Here's Robin with her brand new recip saw cutting through the nails so the door frame will come out easily. She's looking forward to the next demolition project so she can hone her sawing skills.

DOOR JAMB

NAIL

OLD DOOR FRAME

4 Remove the frame from the opening. Danny didn't have any trouble getting the frame out after removing the trim and cutting the nails and screws. The sill was stuck down with caulk, but broke free as Danny tilted the frame.

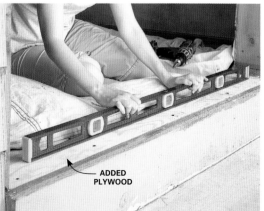

5 Check the sill. Robin was a lot more flexible than Danny, so he let her do most of the low work. Here she's checking the sill area to make sure it's level. They've already added a layer of plywood to raise the door a little.

ADDED PLYWOOD

EXTERIOR MAINTENANCE & REPAIRS

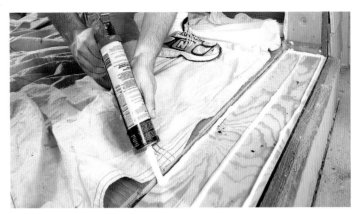

6 Caulk the opening. Danny's done a lot of caulking, so this part was easy. He inspected the bottom of the door frame and did some measuring to be sure the beads of caulk aligned with flat spots on the sill. When Danny finished caulking the sill, he caulked around the perimeter of the opening, too.

7 Set the door frame. Robin and Danny could rest easy now. The door frame slid into the opening as planned and the heavy-lifting part of the job was done.

8 Tack the top corners. Here Robin is trying out her nailing skills. The 16-penny nails proved a bit much, though, so Danny took over the nailing duty.

9 Plumb the hinge side. Robin was a natural with the level, so she's checking to make sure the jamb is plumb while Danny makes adjustments from the inside.

protection from water, but if you install a door that's exposed to the weather, be sure to add a sill pan to protect the subfloor (one brand is Jamsill Guard, jamsill.com; call 800-526-7455 for ordering information) and a metal drip cap over the exterior trim.

Install the new door

With the old door out and the opening prepared, we were ready to install the new door and sidelight. Before we started, I explained to Robin and Danny that our goal was to set the new door frame in the opening and then adjust it with shims until the door fit perfectly. First we removed all the packing material from the new door and hoisted it into the opening to check the fit. The width was a little tight. We didn't have much wiggle room between the siding and the brick molding, but it was obvious we could make it work. So we removed the door unit and Danny applied heavy beads of polyurethane caulk to the sill and exterior

sheathing (**Photos 6 and 7**). Danny and Robin moved the door to the opening and tilted it into place (**Photo 7**). Now we were ready to tack it in and add shims.

Shimming a door is the most critical part of the installation since it's when you tweak the frame to make the door fit perfectly and operate smoothly. I helped Robin and Danny center the top of the door frame with an equal caulk space between the siding and the trim on each side, and then tack the two top corners with 16d galvanized casing nails, letting the heads stick out so we could make adjustments later, if necessary (**Photo 8**).

Next Robin held a level to the hinge-side trim while Danny pried on the frame until the jamb was plumb (**Photo 9**). We drove another nail at the bottom of the hinge-side jamb to hold the frame plumb. With the door temporarily tacked in place, Danny and I headed around through the back door with a couple of bundles of wood shims. I gave him pointers as he wedged pairs of shims behind the hinges and along the top and far side of the frame. The goal was to create an even gap between the door and the frame (**Photo 10**). The key to shimming is to look at the gap between the door and the frame, and then decide how you can wedge the frame to correct any problems. We spent about 45 minutes adjusting shims before we were satisfied with the way the door fit.

Nails through the exterior trim hold the door frame temporarily, but they don't offer enough support to keep the door square over time. For that we still needed to drive 3-in. screws through the jamb and into the wall framing (**Photo 11**). We drove the screws at the shim locations to hold the shims in place and avoid bending the jamb. Then Danny set the nails that we had left sticking out and added nails about 16 in. apart along the exterior trim. After Danny completed this step, he made one final check of the door's fit in case adjustments were needed before we added insulation and reinstalled the interior trim.

> **"I didn't know that shimming a door was such a fussy, time-consuming job."**
> — **Danny**

Add the finishing touches

It was a relief to have the door securely installed. Robin and Danny relaxed, knowing they could lock the door for the night. I didn't have to warn Danny about the dangers of squirting too much expanding foam into the space around the door (**Photo 12**). He'd already learned that the hard way. With the space between the door and the frame well sealed and insulated, we moved to the outside, where we fitted a piece of trim over the door and caulked around the brick molding to seal the exterior. Now all that was left to do was install new interior trim, finish the door and install the new handle and lock.

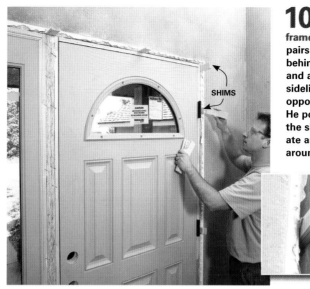

10 **Shim the door frame.** Danny slid pairs of shims behind the hinges and along the sidelight on the opposite side. He positioned the shims to create an even gap around the door.

SHIMS

COUNTERSINK HOLE

3" SCREW

11 **Secure the frame with screws.** After checking to make sure the door was contacting the weather stripping evenly and operating smoothly, Danny drilled countersink holes and drove 3-in. screws through the jamb at each hinge location. To secure the hinge side, he removed one short screw from each hinge and replaced it with a long screw.

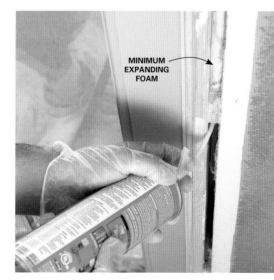

MINIMUM EXPANDING FOAM

12 **Seal the shim space.** Danny was experienced with spray foam, so he handled this task admirably. He managed to fill the space between the jamb and the framing with foam without getting it all over the place.

Question&Answer

FORGET SELF-CLOSING HINGES

I bought a new spring hinge for the service door to my attached garage, but it's not an exact duplicate. I dread the thought of replacing and remortising all three hinges. What are my other options?

Replacement spring hinges are expensive (about $32 per set). But for just a little more money ($48), you can buy a high-quality hydraulic door closer (shown here is Global No. TC2204; $48 from amazon.com). You can find less expensive door closers ($35), but they don't last as long and are less adjustable.

If you have a steel door, don't use the wood screws that come with the unit (they'll pull out after a week). Instead, drill the mounting holes (make sure the drill is level) all the way through the door and mount the unit with hex bolts, nuts and lock washers. Then fine-tune the door's operation as shown.

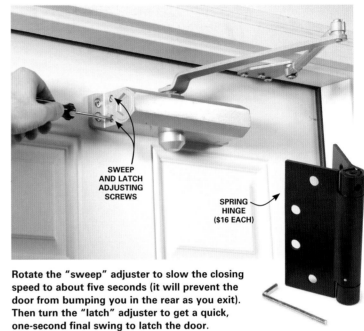

SWEEP AND LATCH ADJUSTING SCREWS

SPRING HINGE ($16 EACH)

Rotate the "sweep" adjuster to slow the closing speed to about five seconds (it will prevent the door from bumping you in the rear as you exit). Then turn the "latch" adjuster to get a quick, one-second final swing to latch the door.

DO-IT-YOURSELF WINDOW SCREENS

I have some aluminum-framed screens that are beyond repair. The hardware store wants a fortune to make new ones. Is there some way I can make new ones myself?

Most home centers sell screen frame kits and rolls of screen. Just cut the rails to the proper size with a hacksaw and slide in the plastic corners. The kits come with the spline to trap the screen in the channel, but you'll have to buy a spline embedding tool (less than $5 at home centers). For simple screens, just follow the directions. However, if your old screens have latches, spring clips or pull tabs, bring one inside and fire up the computer to order the parts you'll need. Have the old screen handy for measurements and to match the hardware to the catalog images at alcosupply.com or blainewindow.com.

FILL BIG GAPS BEFORE CAULKING

I keep filling the control joints in my concrete patio, but the caulk keeps peeling away from both sides of the crack. What's going on and how can I fix it?

The solution is to use a combination of backer rod ($2.50 to $4 for 20 ft. at home centers) and caulk. First remove the caulk that's in the gap. For latex caulk, pour caulk remover (such as Lift Off; about $6 at home centers and hardware stores) over the caulk, let it sit for two hours, then dig out the caulk with a stiff putty knife. For silicone or polyurethane caulk, use mineral spirits. If you're not sure what type of caulk you have, start with the caulk remover. For stubborn sections, give the remover more time to work, then continue scraping. You don't have to remove every last piece of caulk, especially if it's at the bottom of the gap, but the top 1 in. of the crack needs to be cleaned off pretty well.

Use a backer rod with a diameter that's 1/8 to 1/4 in. larger than the crack. Push the rod into the gap so the top is about 1/4 in. below the concrete surface. Fill the gap with caulk, them smooth the caulk with a plastic spoon. Be sure to use a caulk that's formulated for use with concrete (it'll say so on the label).

BACKER ROD IS THE KEY
Insert backer rod into the gap, then run a bead of caulk over the top. For a smooth, even bead, tool the caulk with a plastic spoon.

REPACK THE STEM
With the valve in the off position, loosen the packing nut and slide it toward the handle. Then repack the stem with the Teflon packing cord.

REPACK A STEM SEAL ON A STREET VALVE

The street-side valve at my water meter has been dripping for years. I tightened the stem nut, but it still leaks. The utility wants $40 to shut the water off. Can I repack the stem with the water on?

Yes, you can. But you have to close the valve first. The gate valve will keep water from gushing out of the stem when you repack the nut.

Buy Teflon packing cord at any hardware store or home center. You'll get some water spray once you loosen the packing nut, so move anything you care about away from the meter area.

Most old valves have rust and mineral deposits in the gate valve's receiving groove. That crud can jam the gate and damage the valve. So flush the valve before you crank down on the handle.

GreatGoofs®

Snow job gone wrong

My wife isn't exactly a farm girl. You know, not well acquainted with running machinery. So I was surprised when she called me at work to say she was going to clear the snow out of our driveway with the garden tractor snowblower. I was quite happy to skip snow-blowing in the dark after work.

But when I got home, the driveway was an absolute mess. Weirdly shaped piles of snow were everywhere, along with ruts across the driveway into the lawn—not exactly the bang-up job I'd been hoping for. We plodded through the drifts to rescue the tractor, which was stuck in a snowbank. I climbed aboard and fired it up. My wife got the most incredulous look on her face—she had no idea there was a switch that existed solely to turn on the snowblower.

When the building inspector showed up for the footing inspection, he told me that I needed a crawl space for the addition—not just a footing—meaning I had to dig out the entire area.

I hired an excavator, who showed up with his skid steer and promptly began filling in my hard-dug trench so he could get to the addition area. I not only did all that digging for nothing but also used up my free labor capital getting my friends to help me—and I hadn't even started building anything yet.

Digging into trouble

I was building an addition onto our house and needed to dig a trench for the footings. I enlisted a few friends with shovels, and we worked all day digging out the rocky soil.

Last laugh

My son asked me to help him install a new high-definition roof antenna. I followed him up the extension ladder, carrying everything I needed for the job. Halfway up, I realized that my son had disturbed a hornets' nest behind the gutter, and they were coming out in force to see what caused the rumble. Since it was too late to stop climbing, I plowed right past, with only a couple of stings. But now we were stuck on the roof.

I could see the hornets swarming all around the ladder. We sat on the roof for about an hour, waiting for them to settle down, then I braved the swarm once again (two more stings) on the world's fastest ladder descent. I moved the ladder so my son could get down without getting stung. But later that night, I had the last laugh—me and that spray can of hornet killer.

Hints & Tips for Storage & Organizing

TEMPORARY VALET ROD

We often need temporary clothes-hanging space around the house, so we keep an extra shower tension bar handy. We put it between the jambs in the laundry room door on heavy laundry days. And other times I use it in our bedroom closet to pack for trips or stick it in the closet opening in the guest room/den so overnight guests can hang up their clothes. It's a quick and easy way to gain an extra closet!

SHOWER TENSION BAR

SEE-THROUGH SCREW STORAGE

A lot of people store their screws in an old coffee can. You can't immediately see what's inside, and when you reach in for screws, the points prick your fingers and you're likely to bring up dirt and dust along with the screws. Use a clear water bottle instead. The screws stay clean and you can shake them out one at a time.

SCREW SIZE

HOSE HIDE-A-KEY

Every thief knows that people often hide their spare house key under a doormat or inside a fake rock. Here's a better idea. File down the head of the key (make sure it still works easily in the lock) and then hide it inside the cap of a soaker hose. Brass keys don't rust, and a thief isn't likely to unscrew your hose cap to search for your key.

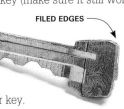

FILED EDGES

PORTABLE THREE-RING WRENCH BINDER

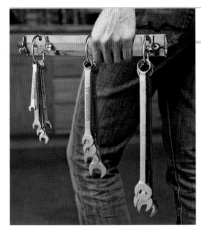

Here's a way to carry your wrenches around with you so you're sure to have the one you need when and where you need it. Use a three-ring binder assembly from an old notebook as a portable wrench organizer. The three rings hold a ton of wrenches, and it's a snap to get them on and off. The binder works great to keep the wrenches handy when you're working in your shop, too. Just drill out the rivets and hang it on some nails to keep everything you need close by.

Hints & Tips for Storage & Organizing

BILL ZUEHLKE

FEMALE ADAPTER

CLEANOUT PLUG

LOW-COST STORAGE TUBES

Storing fishing rods, drill bits, blueprints, maps, cross-country skis and other long, skinny items is a challenge. You can buy special plastic storage tubes, but they're not cheap. Why not make your own for a fraction of the cost? Use PVC pipe, caps, female adapters and cleanout plugs. You can find the parts at any hardware store or home center. Cut the pipe to length with a handsaw or miter saw. Glue an end cap to one end and a female adapter to the other with PVC cement. Twist in a threaded cleanout plug for a cap. If sealing isn't important, you can drill holes in the pipe to make it lighter weight.

A WALL OF STORAGE FOR JOE'S GARAGE

Joe had a lot of stuff in his garage and nowhere to put all of it. Sound familiar? Go to familyhandyman.com and type "garage storage wall" into the search box. You'll get the complete how-to for building the storage wall shown above.

BEFORE

CABINET DOOR BAG BINDER

Here's a handy way to keep paper bags organized and out of the way. Screw cup hooks to the inside of a cabinet door and stretch two screen-door springs ($2 at home centers) between them.

CUP HOOK

BILL ZUEHLKE

WIRE SHELVING "CORRAL"

For years we stored our gift wrap propped against the wall in the hall closet. Of course, some of the rolls would fall over and get lost behind other things or end up wrinkled or torn. Last summer I added wire shelves to the closet and had some shelving left over. Using the plastic shelf clips, I screwed a small section to the closet wall and made a wrapping paper "corral."

OVERHEAD SPRING CLAMPS

If you have a shop in the garage, try this tip from reader Dan Amstutz. Clip all of your spring clamps on the top garage door brace. The clamps are always right at hand whether you're working with the door shut or al fresco (that's with the door open, for those of you who don't speak Garage Italiano).

MOVABLE MUDROOM STORAGE HOOKS

You know that old saying, "If I wanted you to hang your stuff on the floor, I would have put hooks there"? That fit my kids and their backpacks to a "T." Every day after school, they dropped their packs on the floor near the back door, and I tripped over them constantly. We tried regular hooks on the wall, but the kids found it hard to slip the narrow fabric loops over them. Then I installed a towel bar near the door and hung S-hooks from it. The hooks

move around, so it's easy to fit several packs on it at once. It's perfect for hanging up wet hats, scarves and mittens, too. Bring your towel bar along when you buy the S-hooks so you get the right size. I found mine at the hardware store, but the pot rack S-hooks at cooking stores work great, too.

ELECTRICAL BOX TOOL HOLDERS

Does all the little stuff lying around your shop drive you crazy? Junction boxes can do a lot more than hold switches and wiring—they can also help you stay organized! They're inexpensive (50¢ to $2) and they come in different sizes and shapes. Nail or screw them wherever you need handy holders for small tools, tape measures, bottles of glue—almost anything little.

BILL ZUEHLKE

CONVENIENT CORD LABELS

You crawl underneath your desk to unplug something, only to find six different cords—and you have no clue which is the one you're after. Here's a simple idea. Label each cord with a piece of tape. It makes finding the one you need a snap.

Hints & Tips for Storage & Organizing

FLAT COOKWARE ORGANIZER

I found it frustrating to dig through a cabinet jam-packed with baking sheets, cake pans, pizza pans and cutting boards all stacked on top of one another. It was always a chore to find the one I needed. I transformed the cabinet by removing the shelf and screwing in short sections of wire shelving to create vertical dividers. Now I can easily see where everything is located, and I slide out just what I need.

WIRE SHELVING

PVC CURLING IRON HOLSTERS

I hated the messy look of my curling irons lying on the vanity or the toilet tank. They were always in the way, and the cords kept falling into the sink or onto the floor. I solved the problem with PVC pipe. I used hook-and-loop tape to attach 5-in. lengths of 2-in.-diameter pipe to the vanity door to hold my curling irons. I did the same thing with 3-in. pieces of 1-1/2-in.-diameter pipe to hold the cords. Just measure your curling irons to see how long your "holsters" need to be. Let your curling irons cool before you stow them away.

1-1/2" PVC

2" PVC

SPOOL CENTER

I used to keep all my tape, twine and ribbon spools in a drawer. Not only did it look messy, but it wasted a lot of space and made it hard to find things. Last winter I came up with this great organizing idea. I screwed a paper towel holder to the window trim in my craft room and stuck rolls of the things I use most often on the holder. Now I know right where everything is, and I can pull off the amount I need without the spool jumping out of my hand and rolling across the floor.

OUTLET BOX SAFE

3-1/2" REMODELER OUTLET BOX

I love the idea of foiling a crook, and I saw fake wall outlet "safes" online for $10 plus shipping. I made my own for less than $5. All I did was cut a hole in my drywall and install a 3-1/2-in.-deep "remodeler" outlet box. I screwed on a coax cable cover for a convenient little handle. Now I have a secret place to stash cash and jewelry where no thieves would ever think to look. (Unless they read *The Family Handyman* magazine.)

COAX CABLE BOX COVER

Metric Conversions

Use the tables on these two pages to convert the English or "standard" measurements in this book into metric form. In the English system to metric system and Metric system to English system charts below, multiply the number in the first column by the number in the third column to arrive at the conversion number in the middle column.

English system to metric system

To change:	Into:	Multiply by:
Inches	Millimeters	25.4
Inches	Centimeters	2.54
Feet	Meters	0.305
Yards	Meters	0.914
Miles	Kilometers	1.609
Square inches	Square centimeters	6.45
Square feet	Square meters	0.093
Square yards	Square meters	0.836
Cubic inches	Cubic centimeters	16.4
Cubic feet	Cubic meters	0.0283
Cubic yards	Cubic meters	0.765
Pints	Liters	0.473
Quarts	Liters	0.946
Gallons	Liters	3.78
Ounces	Grams	28.4
Pounds	Kilograms	0.454
Tons	Metric tons	0.907

Metric system to English system

To change:	Into:	Multiply by:
Millimeters	Inches	0.039
Centimeters	Inches	0. 394
Meters	Feet	3.28
Meters	Yards	1.09
Kilometers	Miles	0.621
Square centimeters	Square inches	0.155
Square meters	Square feet	10.8
Square meters	Square yards	1.2
Cubic centimeters	Cubic inches	0.061
Cubic meters	Cubic feet	35.3
Cubic meters	Cubic yards	1.31
Liters	Pints	2. 11
Liters	Quarts	1.06
Liters	Gallons	0.264
Grams	Ounces	0.035
Kilograms	Pounds	2.2
Metric tons	Tons	1.1

FRACTIONS AND METRIC EQUIVALENTS

Fractional inches

Inches (in.)	1/64	1/32	1/25	1/16	1/8	1/4	3/8	2/5	1/2	5/8	3/4	7/8
Millimeters (mm)*	0.40	0.79	1.0	1.59	3.18	6.35	9.53	10	12.7	15.9	19.1	22.2
Centimeters (cm)*							0.95	1	1.27	1.59	1.91	2.22

Whole inches (1–12)

Inches (in.)	1	2	3	4	5	6	7	8	9	10	11	12
Millimeters (mm)*	25.4	50.8	76.2	101.6	127	152	178	203	229	254	279	305
Centimeters (cm)*	2.54	5.08	7.62	10.16	12.7	15.2	17.8	20.3	22.9	25.4	27.9	30.5
Meters (m)*												0.30

Selected large measurements

Inches (in.)	36	39.4
Feet (ft.)	3	3-1 /4†
Yard (yd.)	1	1-1/12†
Millimeters (mm)*	914	1,000
Centimeters (cm)*	91.4	100
Meters (m)*	.91	1.00

* Metric values are rounded off. †Approximate fractions.

Also Available from Reader's Digest

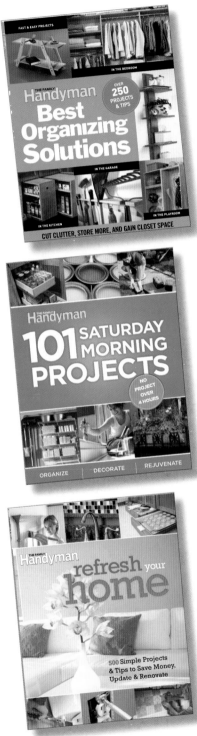

The Family Handyman's Best Organizing Solutions

Be clutter-free in no time with easy do-it-yourself projects for organizing your home from *The Family Handyman*. Includes more than 300 projects and tips for your garage, kitchen and bathrooms, workshop, laundry rooms, closets, and yard.

ISBN 978-1-60652-170-0
$14.95 USA

101 Saturday Morning Projects

From the experts at *The Family Handyman*—the #1 home-improvement magazine—here are more than 100 do-it-yourself projects ideal for every homeowner or apartment dweller. Each project can be completed in a half day or less.

ISBN 978-1-60652-018-5
$14.95 USA

Refresh Your Home

Over 500 resourceful projects and tips to spruce up your home and yard. You'll also find bonus sections on painting, cleaning, and storage as well as a collection of the experts' favorite shortcuts and hints.

ISBN 978-1-60652-201-1
$16.95 USA